SEVEN SPIRITUAL

**A PRACTICAL GUIDE TO THE
FULFILLMENT OF YOUR DREAMS**

Dr. Mushtaq H. Jaafri

Copyright © 1998
MUSHTAQ PUBLISHING COMPANY

First Printing 500 copies, May 1998

SCRIPTURE QUOTATIONS IN THE BEGINNING OF EACH OF THE SEVEN SPIRITUAL LAWS OF NATURE ARE TAKEN FROM THE SPIRITUAL VERSES OF THE HOLY QURAN, TRANSLATED BY SHAIKN MOHAMMAD SARWAR - PUBLISHED BY THE ISLAMIC SEMINARY, P.O. BOX 1115 ELMHURST, N.Y. 11373 U.S.A.

All rights reserved. No part may be reproduced, EXCEPT for the inclusion of brief passages or quotations in a review or article, without any permission from the author or the writer or the publisher.

Editorial & Production:
Type design & Typography: Morris Publishing
Cover designed by: Tracie Walt
Cover artist: Tracie Walt

ISBN: 1-892189-00-3
Library of Congress Catalog Card Number: 98-91343

Published by:
Mushtaq Publishing Company
P.O. Box 4157, San Dimas, California 91773 U.S.A.

Printed in the USA by

MORRIS PUBLISHING

3212 East Highway 30 • Kearney, NE 68847 • 1-800-650-7888

Surely, in Our hands is guidance ...
and to Us belong the hereafter ...
and the wordly life. (Al-Layl 92:2).

— THE HOLY QURAN —

Published By

MUSHTAQ PUBLISHING COMPANY

Dept. 1
919 Sonora Ct.
Box 4157
San Dimas, CA 91773
USA

Printed in the United States Of America

The contents of this book reflect the author's views acquired through his personal experience in the field under discussion. The author is not engaged in rendering any professional medical services. Readers who need medical advice or assistance are advised to seek the services of a medical professional. The publisher, author and writer disclaim any personal or corporate loss or liability resulting from the use or misuse of any information presented herein.

Copyright © 1998 Mushtaq Publishing Company
All rights reserved.

NO PART OF THIS BOOK MAY BE REPRODUCED IN ANY FORM WITHOUT WRITTEN CONSENT OF THE PUBLISHER, EXCEPT BY A REVIEWER WHO MAY QUOTE ANY PASSAGES IN A REVIEW.

A writer or a speaker
can only express his thoughts
about a mortal like himself, but
the holy Quran is the words of the
Supreme Being.
It is said, that reading of the holy Quran,
reflecting upon the meaning of it's verses and
practicing what the holy Quran preaches all are
virtuous deeds.
It simply is not possible to convey in full the
meaning of the verses of the holy Quran. All the
translations of the holy Quran, have fallen far
behind the linguistic beauty of the original
as well as it's ideas.
The English translation of the few select
verses of the holy Quran are meant only to be
a ground work for The Seven Spiritual Laws
of Nature implications of the holy verses.
The holy Quran
is the full text of Divine
guidance for
Man-Kind.

Contents

Acknowledgements xi

Introduction xiii

Chapter 1
    The Law Of Universal Balance!! 1
    Applying The Law Of Universal Balance!! 9

Chapter 2
    The Law Of Harmony And Attraction 11
    Applying The Law Of Harmony And Attraction!! 17

Chapter 3
    The Law Of Cosmic Habit Formation 19
    Applying The Law Of Cosmic Habit Formation 26

Chapter 4
    The Law Of Compensation!! 27
    Applying The Law Of Compensation! 34

Chapter 5
    The Law Of Eternal Sorrow!! 35
    Applying The Law Of Eternal Sorrow!! 41

Chapter 6
    The Law Of Eternal Struggle!! 43
    Applying The Law Of Eternal Struggle 49

Chapter 7
    The Law Of Eternal Change 51
    Applying The Law Of Eternal Change!! 55

Chapter 8
    You're In The Flow Of Abundance!! 57

Chapter 9
    Unlock The Door To A Gold-Mine Of Riches 65
    Seven Major Enemies Of Mankind! 69

Chapter 10
    Use... Master-Key To All Riches Wisely 77

Chapter 11
    Nourish Your Mind With The Seven Positive
        Emotions 93
    The Seven Major Positive Emotions! 100

Chapter 12
    Capitalize On The ... Power Of Your
        Other-Self! 103

Chapter 13
    Increase Your Power By Connecting
        With Others 121

Chapter 14
    Summary and Conclusion 139

About The Author 149

Review Of Literature 153

Ahmad Bay Story...155

Final Words!! 157

Touched By An Angel..162

Letters & Documents 167

Acknowledgements:

I would like to express my deepest gratitude to the many people with whom I've worked to produce ideas that are presented in this unique, one of a kind book, as well as for support needed to complete it.

To Abida Khanam Jaafri, my wife, partner in life, and a very special woman in my life. There can be no richer person than the one who has been blessed with an understanding spouse. Her or his faith in you gives you the necessary support, you need, to press forward toward your own goals in life.

To Lilah, Mustafa, Murtaza and Mujtaba Jaafri, my four children, for being the living expression of The Seven Spiritual Laws Of Nature. I'm indeed, grateful for their unshakable faith and support, and accepting me the way I am and NOT, the way I should be; especially during the past twenty five years, while putting the manuscript of this amazing book together. My wife and children have given me MORE than they received, in ways only a spouse or a father can truly know.

To all my professional associates, present and past who worked with me, and whose encouragements and commitments to the ideas in this new book have given meaning to the WORDS by 'living' them, even when it was impossible and when there seem to be no good reason for doing so.

My very special thanks to Kirsten Bespalec, former publishing manager of Morris Publishing, and all the technical staff, who helped me fulfill my own life-dream of wanting to self-publish a mystical, motivational and inspiring new colorful book, which contains information, ideas, or inspiration and insights which will surely add to reader enjoyment, wisdom or awareness and share my knowledge and insights with others.

Morris publishing provided me with a Publishing Guide instruction booklet. This amazing booklet allowed me to be both author and publisher. I believe that to write a book is an art; to self publish one is business. I also believe that there is more to producing a new book than simple ink on paper. That's why I'm so grateful to Morris Publishing for offering me all the technical, friendly and professional help and a full line of services to assist me with every aspect of Self-Publishing.

And, finally, to all my new readers, I'm, indeed grateful for your courage and commitment to a vision that is awesome, inspiring, lofty, noble and self-transforming.

If this self-knowledge will help change your life around, even in the smallest of ways then, my twenty five years of hard work will have been well rewarded.

Thank you all for supporting my work so enthusiastically.

Introduction:

You are about to become acquainted with a power 'secret' that may CHANGE YOUR LIFE STYLE COMPLETELY, just as it has mine. But, before you and I become involved in this intricate, unique and different way to transform your life, let's have a heart-to-heart talk. I'll talk and you'll listen, okay? A few years ago, through my own stupidity and an offer for a business venture in the Middle East, I lost EVERYTHING that was precious to me; my home, my belongings, and my business. Down on my luck and no place to go to, I began to wander around searching for my self and some answers that would make my own life bearable. I spent much time in local parks and in public libraries because they were FREE and warm. Hoping to find a royal road to riches and fortunes, I joined secret fraternal organizations. Day by day, I began to find myself sinking deeper and deeper into depression. I was totally broke; financially, emotionally, and spiritually. And then, finally, out of desperation, I made some drastic changes!

And the way I made these drastic changes was, that instead of feeling sorry for myself and blaming others for all my misfortune, I decided to totally commit myself to discovering the 'secret' of all human achievements by reading as many books as I could find. My passion, my mission, my obsession had become to find out what was the one 'key' secret of all successful people in all walks of life. I wanted to know what was the difference between me and all other people who were successful.

I wanted to know the one FOUNDATIONAL key to all of human success both in their personal as well in professional life.

So, I began to search for the answers ...

I read as many books as I could possibly find on human development personal motivation, and in the field of self-help. I also read books on the Science Of Mind, in the Metaphysical field and books on ALL religions. I spent year after year reading, studying and understanding the one common denominator or the one fundamental 'key' secret to all human achievements.

But, you know, still, the great 'secret' kept just a jump ahead of me! It was amazing that the ultimate power 'secret' was mentioned no fewer than a hundred times through out each great book I read, but nevertheless; it did take me over twenty five years of constant search to uncover the suggestions and the clues that each author was giving me. One of the reasons it took me so long to uncover this 'secret' was that it had not been directly named, for it seemed to work more successfully when it was merely unfolded and left in sight where those who are ready for it and searching for it, may pick it up.

So you can imagine the distress, the frustrations, and the agony I was going through for not being able to put all the parts together.

And then; finally, in the hour of my greatest distress, I found my greatest asset in the discovery and revelation of my "OTHER-SELF", the "GOD-SELF" -- by reading a philosophy of individual achievement by utilizing The Seven Spiritual Laws Of Nature.

This particular philosophy I read said, that each one of us have TWO DISTINCT PERSONALITIES within us.

One is the kind of personality that we see when we stand in front of a mirror. THIS IS KNOWN AS THE "PERSONAL-SELF"! This is the "Self" that usually brings us misery, sickness, poverty, unhappiness and all the BAD things of life we do not desire or want.

And then; other is the kind of personality that we NEVER see when we stand in front of a mirror but; rather we 'assume' or FEEL this personality inside of us. THIS IS KNOWN AS THE "GOD-SELF"! This is the "God-Self", inside of us that brings us health, happiness, peace, and prosperity and all the GOOD things of life we do desire and want. This is the "Self" that let's us recognize within ourselves a greater potentials and to use them to enrich the quality of our daily lives. This is the "Self" that is infinitely creative, infinitely loving and totally BALANCE. It is the "Self", when discovered fulfills consciousness. A few throughout history have become saints through this ultimate experience of their MINDS, but this is not the aim or goal — to live life more productively by greater participation in it is the aim or goal. Truly, if all the world understood The Seven Spiritual Laws Of Nature and then lived by them, indeed, all the problems of the earth would be solved and peace, love, harmony, and prosperity would be the experience of all human kind! All of creation, everything that exists in the physical world, is the result of the manifestation of The Seven Spiritual Laws Of Nature, because these are the SAME principles that nature uses to create everything in material existence—everything we can see, hear, smell, taste or touch.

Now let's go over The Seven Spiritual Laws Of Nature and see how we can apply them in our lives.

Chapter 1
The Law Of Universal Balance!!

"By the sun and it's noon-time brightness, by the moon when it follows the sun, by the day when it brightens the earth, by the night when it covers the earth with darkness, by the heavens and that (power) which established them, by the earth and that (power) which spread it out and by the MIND and that (power) which designed it and inspired it with knowledge of evil and piety, those who purify their MIND will certainly have everlasting happiness and those who corrupt their MINDS will certainly be deprived (of happiness). (Al-Shams 91:2).

— THE HOLY QURAN —

The first spiritual law of nature is called the Law Of Universal Balance. This law is based on the fact that nature uses this law to keep a perfect harmony among other planets. It is this law of the Universal Balance that provides the (power) that gravitates all bodies toward the center of the earth.

Through this Law of Universal Balance a perfect system of "BALANCE" exists among all stars, planets, all matter, the sun, the moon, night, day, summer, and winter throughout the universe. By this Law Of Nature, each is 'fixed' with it's own position and NEVER interfere with others as they 'move' through time and space. Without this "BALANCE", there would be constant chaos through collisions of stars and planets.

Although, this Law Of Nature is primarily designed to 'control' and run this universe, nevertheless; our CREATOR HAS GIVEN US THE PRIVILEGE AND THE POWER TO AFFECT, USE, AND HARMONIZE WITH THE LAW OF THE UNIVERSAL BALANCE.

There is a beauty of NATURE all around us. Nature operates according to a 'perfect' plan, and the plan itself is a beauty. Look around you! Beauty exists everywhere. To fully understand just "how" our universe operates according to a perfect plan, we must first recognize, relate, assimilate and then apply this Law Of Universal Balance to our own lives. In a psychic nut-shell then, The First Spiritual Law Of Nature allows TWO PERSONALITIES to work together as partners. When we realize that our true Self, is one of pure potentiality, we then align with the (power) that manifests everything in the universe. When you discover your true Self (and know who you are), in that knowing itself is the ability to fulfill any dream you have. It draws people to you, and it also draws things to you that you desire and want. It magnetizes people, situations, and also circumstances to support your dreams. (This is also called the support from the laws of nature).

How can we apply the Law Of Universal Balance, to our lives? If you want to enjoy the benefits of the Laws Of Universal Balance, if you want to make full use of the creativity which is inherent in the Laws of nature, then you have to have access to it. One way to access the Law Of Balance is through understanding just how this universal law operates according to a perfect plan in our Solar System.

In our 'Solar System', our planet Earth and Nine other Planets are constantly revolving around the SUN. As they travel, a perfect system of 'Balance' exists among these planets, never interfering with other planets, as they perform their duties 'fixed' permanently in a position until their intended time Herein lies; the hidden 'secret' of applying the Laws Of Universal Balance in our own lives. Let me explain!

In our 'Solar System', our planet Earth and Nine other planets are constantly traveling around the SUN.

In our 'Mental System', all kind of thoughts (both negative and positive) are constantly traveling around our MINDS. Now, much like the planets that occupy a certain 'fixed' position in the 'Solar System', the same way, all negative thoughts occupy one 'fixed' position while all positive thoughts occupy another 'fixed' position in our 'Mental System'.

In the 'Solar System', these planets NEVER interfere with each other because of the Law Of Universal Balance, the very same way, our negative thoughts and our positive thoughts will NEVER interfere with each other in our 'Mental System'. Get it!

One of the profound truths about our own MIND is the fact that no two thoughts can occupy the MIND AT THE SAME TIME.

So—since only ONE thought must occupy the MIND at any given time, and since it will not interfere with ANY other thoughts in the MIND, we can 'deliberately' KEEP OUR OWN MIND "FIXED" ON THE CIRCUMSTANCES OF LIFE THAT WE DESIRE OR WANT—AND—COMPLETELY IGNORE ALL OTHER CIRCUMSTANCES OF LIFE WE DO NOT DESIRE OR WANT. CAN IT BE DONE? YES! HOW? Through a strictest self-discipline.

This is the one foundational 'key' to the proper use of the Law Of Universal Balance.

UNDERSTAND AND ADOPT TO THIS TRUTH, OR PERISH, IS THE WARNING!

Through self-discipline you may 'think' yourself INTO or OUT of any circumstances of life. Self-discipline will help you to 'control' your own mental attitude. Your mental attitude may help you to MASTER every conceivable circumstance of life, and that (power) will convert every adversity, every defeat, every failure into an 'asset' of equivalent scope.

If you keep at it, a very wonderful thing is going to happen. Your dominating thoughts will SEND OUT psychic 'energy' and they are united on a psychic level WITH ALL OTHER MINDS ON EARTH who are operating on the SAME energy level, and thus; guide you toward the right people, the right opportunities that will make your desires and wants a reality.

If you applied and then lived by The First Spiritual Law Of Nature, you'll always be confident about your future, regardless of what is happening at the 'moment', KNOWING that the very SAME (power) that controls and runs this universe is ALSO working on your behalf to direct your life FOR GOOD ONLY.

The (power) of The Law Of Universal Balance, has been acknowledged since the beginning of recorded history, however; the SIMPLICITY of The spiritual laws has frequently caused to be over-looked. That is why, most people shy away from even attempting to apply these simple yet, highly effective, life-changing spiritual laws. I've been personally applying this first spiritual law of nature in my own life for the last twenty five years. I can honestly tell you that it really does work. I have personally used it to pull myself out of MANY tailspins I was in during the last twenty five years. During this time period, I have used this (power) to over-come many, many financial crisis as well as personal and emotional problems.

The affluence of the universe—the lavish display and abundance of the universe—is an 'expression' of the creative Mind of Nature. The more tuned in you are to the Mind of Nature, the more you have ACCESS to its 'infinite', unbounded creativity. But - first, you HAVE to go beyond the "TURBULENCE" of your inner 'dialogue' to CONTROL with that (power), abundant, affluent, infinite, creative Mind. And then, you create the possibility to 'connect with that (power) controls and runs this universe.

Finally, let me say this:

If you learn just one lesson only, from The First Spiritual Law Of Nature, let it be this, that from this day forward, you 'accept' EACH AND EVERY MOMENT—"As Is"—and NOT as it should be. Just think about this for a moment! Once you recognize this 'truth' that each daily moment "Is As Is" because the whole universe "Is As Is", you then begin to let your personal Self work in harmony with your true Self (God-Self). Once you do, you then allow the SAME (power) of the universe that controls and runs it to "direct" YOUR own life for good.

There is no separation between you and this (power) of the universe. The more you "experience" your own true Self, the CLOSER you are to that (power) of the universe. It draws people to you, and it also draws things that you desire and want in life to you. You enjoy bond with people, and people enjoy bond with you—your (power) is that of bonding, a bonding that comes ONLY from knowing your own true Self (Other-Self).

There are two things that I want you to know about you. If you understand these two things and take them to heart, your own life will NEVER be the same. I guarantee it.

First, you have a special and unique "talent" to give to others: Now — please understand that I'm not saying to praise or glorify you in any way, shape or form. (Unless it happens to be true in your case), I remember, I had a very hard time accepting this (truth) that I HAVE A SPECIAL AND UNIQUE TALENT TO GIVE TO OTHERS. I kept saying to myself Yeh — Sure, "I have a "talent." I almost threw the book out of the window, and I tell you the why? Because; I was just am immigrant from Pakistan, who couldn't speak a word of English, and had very hard time getting admission in some of the reputable Colleges and Universities in the United States of America. But, perhaps the biggest proof of the validity of this (power) of The First Spiritual Law Of Nature came by writing the manuscript of this book to share with you.

It will not surprise me one bit, if that (power) of the universe makes this a best seller in the world. I have seen it happen more than once.

Please understand, that I don't tell all this to impress you! I tell you because, it impresses me! If a person like me with no special talent and with all these handicaps can learn these spiritual laws of nature, so can you, I guarantee it.

So — the very first thing I want you to know about your self is, that you HAVE a special and unique "talent" to GIVE TO OTHERS. In fact this special "talent" is so unique that ONLY YOU CAN DO IT BETTER THAN ANYONE ELSE IN THE WHOLE WORLD, Just think of it! "You have a "talent" that is so unique that there is no one else alive on this planet Earth that has the SAME talent", or that of expression of that talent.

Furthermore; there is a unique NEED for your special "talent", and when this need is MATCHED with the creative expression of your unique "talent", that is when you 'ignite' the spark in the creative MIND of nature, and thus; helps you access it's infinite, unbounded creativity. Expressing your special and unique "talent" to fulfill your own needs, could very well create an unlimited wealth and abundance for life. Know this: Every adversity you face in course of your life-time, no matter how unpleasant, no matter how uncalled for, is a step forward toward your own life's aim or goal. ALL YOU HAVE TO DO IS TO CAPITALIZE ON YOUR OWN INHERENT GOD-GIVEN SPECIAL AND UNIQUE TALENT. THAT'S ALL.

The second thing I want you to know about yourself is (and this is very important) that you HAVE a definite major goal or purpose in your own life — and WHEN YOU BLEND YOUR SPECIAL AND UNIQUE "TALENT" WITH SERVICE TO OTHERS, THAT IS WHEN YOU EXPERIENCE YOUR OWN TRUE-SELF!

In other words, you HAVE a 'mission' in your life for which only YOU were chosen to fulfill it. Think about this a moment! Your own mission, mainly deals with service to humanity — to serve other fellow human beings.

Now — here is the bottom line!

You'll have to find your own purpose in life and, you have to find your 'mission' on your own and then find ways to fulfill that purpose or 'mission' in your life.

How do you do that? Well, the whole purpose of these seven spiritual laws of nature is to HELP YOU FIND YOUR AIM OR GOAL OR MISSION IN YOUR LIFE AND THEN TO FULFILL IT. It took me more than twenty five years to find my own purpose and mission in life, which is to help YOU find yours. All I ask is that you have an open MIND. That's all.

Applying The Law Of Universal Balance!!

I will put the law of Universal Balance into effect by making a commitment to take the following steps:

(1) I will get in touch with the spiritual law of the Universal Balance by taking time each day to 'fix' my own MIND "ON" the things I desire and want in life, and "OFF" the things I do not desire and want in my life.

(2) I will take time each day to be more tuned in to the mind of nature, and to have more access to it's infinite, unbounded huge, creativity and to silently witness the intelligence within every living thing. Spending time in nature will also give me access to the qualities inherent in the law of Universal Balance.

(3) I will begin my day with the statement, "Today, I'm Successful, the door before me is open". Throughout this day, as I go about my business I will remind myself that I will accept each moment AS IS — and NOT AS IT SHOULD BE.

(4) I will be in the flow of abundance by following the world's first Computer-Like Flow Chart to reprogram my own MIND for success using Cutting-Edge Technology for success. I will turn seven major negative Emotions into Positive Anticipations for peace-of-mind.

Chapter 2
The Law Of Harmony And Attraction

"The creation of the heavens and the earth, the alternation of nights and days, the ship that sail in the sea for the benefit of people, the water that (God) sends from the sky to revive the dead earth where (God) has scattered all kinds of animals, the winds of all directions and the clouds rendered for service between the sky and the earth, are all evidence (of God's existence) for those who use their reason." (Al-Baqarah).

— THE HOLY QURAN —

The second spiritual law of nature is called the LAW OF HARMONY AND ATTRACTION. The basis for this second spiritual law is that the LAW OF HARMONY AND ATTRACTION, simply translate everything into their own counter-part.

This law is based on the fact that nature uses this law to PRODUCE THINGS AFTER THEIR OWN KIND. For an example, a seed of an oak tree will produce an oak tree, just as surely the seed of a pine tree will produce another pine tree. Through this spiritual law of nature, an animal will produce another animal, and a human will produce after their own kind.

How can we apply the Law of Harmony And Attraction to our lives? If you want to enjoy the benefits of the Law of Harmony and attraction, if you want to make full use of the creativity which is inherent in this law of nature, then you have to have access to it. One way to access the law of harmony and attraction is through understanding just how "LIKE ATTRACT".

Through this second spiritual law of nature, all 'thoughts' (whether negative or positive is immaterial) will be translated into their own counter-parts. In other words, 'thoughts' of riches, abundance, happiness, wealth, peace and prosperity attract their own counterparts, just as surely as the 'thoughts' of poverty, suffering, pain, disappointments, sorrows, frustrations, will attract their own counter-parts.

Likewise; 'thoughts' of Fear, Hate, Jealousy, Superstition, Greed Revenge and anger will attract their own counter-parts, just as surely as the 'thoughts' (emotions) Desire, Faith, Love, Hope, Caring, Romance and Enthusiasm, will produce their own counterparts. Translated into daily living, a person who is struggling financially should be taught that by 'reversing' his or her own 'thoughts' or emotions, from negative to positive and from poverty to prosperity they will surely begin attracting to them individuals and or opportunities or circumstances that will help then prosper. A person who is lonely and has a feeling of being unloved should begin to 'think' of themselves as a person WHO IS ALREADY LOVED, because they are a person who is capable of giving much love to another person. This second spiritual law of nature explains 'why' most people go through life being unhappy and poor because their dominating 'thoughts' and or emotions are "ON" these circumstances of life.

I earnestly believe that a part of most important work of anyone engaged professionally in the self-help field, is to explain the preceding to people — to make them understand that their own MINDS are like magnets, ATTRACTING back to them the nature of their own dominating 'thoughts' and emotions on a daily basis through the Law of Harmony and Attraction.

When you allow your MIND to Fear poverty or and other negative thoughts or emotions, and once they take hold of your MIND then, the law of Harmony any Attraction makes that a reality. Why? Because, the MIND is a very impartial thing, it will work on whatever you 'feed', whether negative or positive is immaterial. It is your duty to 'guard' against ANY negative 'thoughts' or emotions. Making sure, that ONLY positive 'thoughts' or emotions always dominate your own mind, at ALL TIMES AND AT ALL COSTS. It's a true statement that your LIFE IS WHAT YOUR OWN THOUGHTS AND EMOTIONS MAKE IT, This is the second spiritual law! By the same token: when your dominating 'thoughts' and emotions are "ON" the things you desire and want in life, and when you constantly 'feed' your own MIND with positive, creative, universally inspired 'thoughts' and emotions then, the second law of nature takes over and makes them a reality.

THE VERY SAME POWER THAT CONVERTS AN ACRON INTO AN OAK TREE AND A CATERPILLAR INTO A MAGNIFICENT BUTTERFLY IS AT YOUR DISPOSAL TO WORK ON YOUR BEHALF BY THE SECOND LAW OF HARMONY AND ATTRACTION! Now — how does all this work as far as the daily living of a person? Well, my answer: People who 'think' of their lives in terms of poverty or lack, are operating consciously on this energy-vibration frequency, hence, the chronic poverty thinker is attracted to other poverty thinkers, as they are attracted to him.

Conversely, prosperity thinkers attract and are attracted by other prosperity thinkers in which each helps the other upward in financial matters, while the poverty thinkers get together only to constantly complain how hard times are. In a psychic nut-shell then, bad time thinkers attract bad times, and good-time thinkers attract good-time.

Finally, let me say this:

If you learn just only one lesson from the second spiritual law of Harmony and Attraction, let it be this, that when a person comes to himself or herself, and discovers his or her true Self, the revelation is usually due to a great sorrow or perhaps a failure in a business venture, or due to some physical affliction beyond his or her control. I AM INCLINED TO BELIEVE THAT THE TRUE-SELF REVEALS ITSELF THROUGH "SILENCE" MORE READILY THAN THROUGH THE NOISES OF OUR MAD RUSH TO ACCUMULATE MATERIAL THINGS.

I'm also moved to believe that this 'experience' of the true Self is available ONLY to those who properly interpret and relate to this second spiritual law of nature known as Harmony and Attraction. Due to my one and only great sorrow, due to the failure in the business venture in the Middle East, I discovered the NEW way to my own soul, through this 'experience' of the Inner-Most level of the MIND.

ALL THOSE WHO HAVE EXPERIENCED IT INTUITIVELY, AGREE WITH ME THAT IT IS AN EXPERIENCE WHERE ONE HAS BECOME ONE WITH STARS, NATURE, ALL THINGS LIVING AND THE UNIVERSE.

This 'experience' can only be described as an 'experience' in which one discovers that they are ultimately one with all things as all things are one with them. This universal oneness within oneself may last only a few seconds when 'experienced' as a MIND expansion experience but; it's effect, even if 'experienced' only once in a person's life time remains the major influence or criteria "Identity-Structure", in the individual.

When YOU discover your own true Self, and when you know who you really are, in that knowing itself is the ability to fulfill any desire you have.

There is one thing that I want you to know about you. If you truly understand and take it to heart, you will never be the same person again. " ONLY you have been given the (power) and the privilege to 'harness' the VERY SAME law of nature that converts a tiny SEED into a magnificent oak tree, to shape YOUR own destiny here on earth". Why? You may ask: Well — for one thing, just for having LIVED this life as a human being. What other reason do you need? Remember, YOU are a very superior individual, with a definite special and unique 'talent' to give to others. ALL YOU HAVE TO DO IS TO APPLY THE SECOND SPIRITUAL LAW OF HARMONY AND ATTRACTION CONSISTENTLY: It will surely place you in favor of people, situations, circumstances or anything else you may need, EVERY TIME.

DON'T EXPECT YOUR LOGICAL REASONINGS (no matter how sound they appear to be at the moment) GIVE YOU THE ANSWERS, EXPECT YOUR OWN INTUITIVE MIND TO GIVE YOU THE ANSWERS. How? By following the world's first Computer-Like Flow Chart to reprogram your MIND for success using Cutting-Edge Technology for success, and eliminating the seven major negative emotions from your MIND for good, and feeding the seven major positive emotions into the MIND at all times and at all costs.

This is the price you MUST pay for everlasting happiness.

If the second spiritual law of Harmony And Attraction is so powerful then, why so few avail themselves all the benefits of this universal law. My answer is: The simplicity of the second law of nature has frequently caused to be over-looked. The more you 'experience' yourself — YOUR TRUE-SELF — the 'closer' you are to the (power) of the universe. This (power) draws people to you, and it also draws things to you through Harmony & Attraction.

Applying The Law Of Harmony And Attraction!!

I will put the law of Harmony and Attraction into effect by making a commitment to take the following steps:

(1) I will take time each day to be 'silent', to just BE. I will sit alone and read HOLY BOOKS (such as QURAN) at least twice a day for approximately thirty minutes in the morning and thirty minutes in the evening.

(2) I will take time each day to commune with nature and to silently 'witness' the intelligence within every living thing. I will sit 'silently' and watch a sunset, of listen to the sound of running water, or simply smell the scent of a flower. I will watch the birds fly, fish to swim in the ecstasy of my own 'silence'.

(3) I will make a list of all my desires. I will carry this list with me where ever I go. I will look at this list before I go into my 'silence'. I will look at it before I go to sleep at night. I will look at it when I wake up in the morning.

(4) I will remind myself to practice "Present-moment" awareness in all my actions. I will accept the present moment "As-Is" and not "As-It-Should-Be". I will refuse to allow negative 'thoughts' and emotions to consume and dissipate the quality of my attention in the present 'moment'.

Chapter 3
The Law Of Cosmic Habit Formation

"Praise is only for (GOD), the Lord of the Universe, the All-Compassionate, the All-Merciful, the Master of the Day of Judgment (has all the exalted attributes and) deserves all praise. (Al-Fatihah 2:1)

— THE HOLY QURAN —

The third spiritual law of nature is called the LAW OF COSMIC HABIT FORMATION. The basis for this third spiritual law is that our 'Creator' (GOD), CREATED everything for the over-all purpose of this universe. Let me explain! SUN WAS CREATED TO PRODUCE DAY, PLANETS WERE CREATED TO REVOLVE AROUND THE SUN, MOON TO FOLLOW NIGHTS, SUMMER WITH WINTER, WATER TO FLOW THROUGH GRAVITY.

And then, all of these creations were engineered and designed to 'confine' to a COSMIC HABIT. It was intended that all these creations MUST follow that same, set Cosmic Habit. Through this Cosmic Habit-Formation, the SUN was risen, and the SUN was set, night followed the day, all 'seasons' of the year followed each other. Then, each one of these creations was set in a 'definite' motion, and each remained in that definite motion or 'state', until they all produce a very DEFINITE 'pattern'. This definite PATTERN was taken over by the COSMIC HABIT FORMATION, which in turn, produce the ENERGY necessary to keep the momentum going until it's intended time and space.

Through this third spiritual law of nature, a perfect SYSTEM of balance exists in the universe, where the SUN, the MOON, DAY, NIGHT, SUMMER and WINTER perform their duties, while each travel with balance and harmony like a clock work. How can we apply the Law of Cosmic Habit Formation to our lives? If you want to enjoy the benefits of the Law Of Cosmic Habit Formation, if you want the full use of the infinite (power) and the creativity which is inherent in this third law of nature, then you have to have access to it. One way to access the law of Cosmic Habit Formation is through understanding just how our own HABITS are FORMED.

Our 'dominating' THOUGHTS (whether negative or positive is immaterial), repeated over-and-over again, "SET" a very definite PATTERN in our own MIND. This PATTERN then, is taken over by the third spiritual law of nature, and makes that PATTERN a reality, by every mean possible, through the Law Of The Cosmic Habit Formation.

Very simply stated then, a loving 'thought' or emotion produces one type of 'energy' or frequency (PATTERN), while a hateful 'thought' or emotion produces another type of frequency or 'energy' (PATTERN). A poverty thought is of one frequency, while a prosperous 'thought' is another frequency (energy).

By realizing these known facts, we can then apply this third Law of nature in our own lives through our own choice. We can simply decide to 'choose' the kind of 'thoughts' we want to associate with, repeat them often UNTIL THEY PRODUCE A DEFINITE PATTERN,

The Seven Spiritual Laws of Nature

AND ARE TAKEN OVER BY THE THIRD SPIRITUAL LAW OF NATURE.

Through this third spiritual law of nature, our MIND reaches the SAME 'greater' (power) of the universe to acquire the very same 'energy' that keeps all planets in 'motion', to make our own desires and wants a reality. The most effective way to apply this third spiritual law of nature is through what is commonly known in the self-help field is, "Auto-Suggestion". An Auto suggestion is simply saying something to your self over and over again. When you repeat something to yourself (whether consciously or unconsciously is immaterial) over and over again, you are applying Auto-Suggestion or Self-Suggestion principle. The key to remember is that Auto-Suggestion is the one and only method to 'activate' the switch (so to speak) of your own MIND that will produce the necessary PATTERN to be recognized, and taken over by the LAW OF COSMIC HABIT FORMATION to make your each and every desire and want a reality.

Now — much like the SUN, the MOON, SUMMER, WINTER, DAY and NIGHT are engineered and designed to 'confine' to the very same daily PATTERN, through the third spiritual law of COSMIC HABIT FORMATION, the same way, our DOMINATING THOUGHTS (whether negative or positive is immaterial) 'repeated' over and over again to ourselves by our selves produce a definite PATTERN through this third spiritual law of nature. This definite PATTERN in our own MINDS then, is taken over by the same spiritual law of nature the converts an acorn into an oak tree, and keeps a perfect SYSTEM of balance among all planets, causes the water to flow, birds to fly, fish to swim and grass to grow, helps us also to convert our own dominating 'thoughts' and emotions into their our counter-parts by every mean possible.

Very simply stated then, the third spiritual laws of nature goes something like this:

"Whatever a person 'thinks' on the conscious level of the MIND enters into the second level of the mind called the "Personal Sub-Conscious", or the 'memory bank' of the MIND". Here; over a period of time, a "thought-accumulation" build ... a thought accumulation of both positive (winning), and negative (failure), thoughts in the MIND. It is estimate, that ninth-tenth of a person's conscious 'reaction' to events in daily living, from the most major occurrences to the most trivial occurrences are based upon what a person has "come-to-expect" as a result of a (here's the main key) <u>COMPUTER-LIKE</u> feedback to the conscious MIND from the "personal Sub-Conscious" memory-bank.

The 'secret' to the understanding of this third spiritual laws of nature lies in the fact, that whatever YOU 'think' every day goes into second level of the MIND, where over a period of time, a "thought-accumulation" builds, which in turn sets-up a definite PATTERN in the CONSCIOUS MIND, which is picked up by that (power) the COSMIC HABIT FORMATION through the (power) of the third law of nature.

WE ARE HERE LAYING THE FOUNDATION FOR THE PRESENTATION OF THE FACT OF GREAT IMPORTANCE TO THE PERSON WHO DOES NOT UNDERSTAND WHY SOME PEOPLE APPEAR TO BE LUCKY, WHILE OTHERS OF EQUAL OR GREATER ABILITY, TRAINING, EXPERIENCE, AND BRAIN CAPACITY, SEEM DESTINED TO RIDE WITH MISFORTUNE.

This fact may be explained by the statement that every human being has the ability to COMPLETELY influence and CONTROL his or his MIND. Nature has 'endowed' us with absolute CONTROL over but one thing and THAT IS OUR OWN THINKING!

Every human being in this world, has been given that (power) to fully and completely CONTROL his or her MIND. The only way you COMPLETELY CONTROL YOUR OWN MIND is by simply CONTROLLING your own THINKING.

And, with this control, obviously, every person may <u>OPEN</u> his or her MIND to the TRAMP 'thought-impulses', which are being released by OTHER minds — or — <u>CLOSE</u> the doors 'tightly' and admit ONLY 'thought-impulses' of his or her CHOICE! Here your self-control will come to your rescue. This fact — coupled with the additional fact that BY CONTROLLING YOUR OWN THINKING, YOU CAN CONTROL YOUR OWN MIND — leads us very near to the principle by which you can produce a definite PATTERN, that is easily recognizable BY THE GREATER (POWER) OF THE UNIVERSE.

REMEMBER THIS: You may 'control' your own MIND. You have that (power) to 'feed' it with whatever 'thought, emotion, feeling' YOU choose. CHOOSE TO FEED ONLY POSITIVE THOUGHTS, EMOTIONS, FEELINGS, AT ALL TIMES, AND AT ALL COSTS. By applying this third spiritual law of nature, you are 'engaged' in trying to help 'shut-off' the flow of negative 'impulses-of-thoughts' — and to AID in voluntarily INFLUENCE your Sub-Conscious Mind, through POSITIVE impulses of DESIRES, GOALS or AIM in your life, by producing a definite PATTERN that can be taken over by the spiritual law of COSMIC HABIT FORMATION. You either CONTROL your own MIND (by controlling your own thinking), or YOUR MIND CONTROLS YOU. THERE IS NO HALF WAY COMPROMISE. AS a human being, we control NOTHING in the sphere of life, EXCEPT; our own thinking. This prerogative of being able to have our own thinking under our own control GIVES us the full and complete and un-challengeable PRIVILEGE to CONTROL our own MIND, and almost all other circumstances which AFFECT our own lives.

Before, we begin together, the study of the fourth spiritual law of nature — may I offer one brief suggestion which may provide the 'clue' by which a "Miracle", may be recognized. The 'clue', is simply this: "By giving us the CONTROL over our own 'thinking', our "CREATOR" (GOD) intended this to be a priceless 'asset', because; OUR OWN MIND IS THE ONE AND ONLY MEANS BY WHICH WE MAY PLAN OUR OWN LIVES AND LIVE IT AS WE MAY CHOOSE." Our CREATOR (GOD), gave us complete right to CONTROL our own 'thinking' and along with this profound RIGHT, the REWARD for our exercising the RIGHT, and terrible penalties for failure to exercise it. Here then, is the "Miracle"!

YOUR PRIVILEGE TO TAKE FULL AND COMPLETE POSSESSION OF YOUR OWN MIND, SIMPLY BY KEEPING YOUR OWN MIND SO BUSILY ENGAGED IN "THINKING" OF YOUR OWN DESIRES, AIMS OR GOAL IN LIFE THAT (LITERALLY) NO TIME IS LEFT FOR YOU TO "THINK" OF ANYTHING THAT YOU DO NOT DESIRE OR WANT IN LIFE. (This is what you MUST do.).

Verily, this "Miracle, is so powerful, that those who eventually discover it, will receive with it the means of recognizing and bringing into their services of that (power) mentioned in the previous three spiritual laws of nature. Truly, that (power) is now lie doormat, awaiting your recognition and CALL to service. But, let me be perfectly honest with you, this is ONLY one half of the PASSWORD of that "Miracle". The other half MUST be added to this half.

In the next chapter, the other half of the PASSWORD will be revealed to you. And, when you recognize it, appropriate it, and begin to transmute it into a full life of your own making. Remember this: "You may CONTROL your own MIND". "You have that (power) to 'feed' it whatever 'thoughts', emotions, feelings you choose!

Applying The Law Of Cosmic Habit Formation

I will put this law of Cosmic Habit Formation into effect by making a commitment to take the following steps:

(1) I will get in touch with the third spiritual law of nature by taking time each day to TAKE FULL AND COMPLETE CONTROL OF MY OWN MIND, BY SIMPLY CONTROLLING MY OWN "THINKING".

(2) I will be in the flow of abundance by following the world's first COMPUTER-LIKE flow chart to reprogram my own MIND for success using Cutting-Edge Technology for success. I will completely 'eliminate' all negative emotions from my MIND. I will 'feed' all positive emotions into my MIND at all times and at all costs.

(3) I will take time each day to read my own religion's HOLY BOOK at least twice a day for approximately thirty minutes in the morning and thirty minutes in the evening.

(4) Today I will witness the 'Choices' I make in each moment. I will try to make the 'Choice' of CONTROLLING my own MIND by simply CONTROLLING each and every 'thought' that ENTERS my own MIND. And in the mere witnessing of these "Choices", I will bring them to my 'conscious' awareness. I will know that the best way to prepare for ANY 'moment' in the FUTURE is to fully CONTROL my PRESENT 'thinking'.

Chapter 4
The Law Of Compensation!!

"You (GOD) alone do We worship and from you (GOD) alone do We seek assistance. Guide us to the right path, the path of those to whom You (GOD) granted blessings, not the path of those who are subject to Your violent anger or those who have gone astray". (Al-Fatihah 2:1)

— THE HOLY QURAN —

The fourth spiritual law of nature is called the LAW OF COMPENSATION:

The basis of this fourth spiritual law is that nature REWARDS individuals in exact proportion to their own just efforts but, nature demands that we put forth our own individual efforts first, before we can expect or demand to receive any rewards.

In other words; we MUST do our part FIRST - and then, the fourth spiritual law of nature will do the rest for us.

As an example, a farmer, digs the land, fertilizes it, sows the desired 'seeds', and waters the ground or field for months and months without any sure fire guarantees of ever receiving any crops from whatever he planted but; once the farmer digs the land, plants the seeds and does his job of whatever has to be done then, this fourth spiritual law of Compensation takes over.

Once the farmer has done his part then, he is usually rewarded a hundred or perhaps a thousand fold for each 'seed' that he planted or sowed in the field without ever expecting any direct or immediate return for sure.

NATURE DEMANDS THAT WE PERFORM OUR DUTIES FIRST. But our just part, without expecting an immediate or direct reward or compensation FIRST, then of course; we are bountifully rewarded. How can we apply the fourth spiritual Law Of Compensation, to our lives?. If you want to enjoy the benefits of the Law Of Compensation, if you want to make full use of the creativity which is inherent in the Law Of Compensation, then you have to have access to it. One way to access the Law Of Compensation is through the understanding of the principle of "Going the extra mile". "Through this spiritual law of nature, ALL INDIVIDUALS will be rewarded for their just efforts but; nature demands that we should 'give', or render a useful service, BEFORE expecting to get something in return".

In it's simplest form - this fourth spiritual Laws Of Nature works something like this:

People in sales profession, for example, can utilize this Law of nature by making specific numbers of calls daily, making full and complete presentation of their product or service, being focused in the field, keeping a positive mental attitude no matter what and putting forth their diligent efforts FIRST, before expecting any rewards and always going the extra mile in the field, once a sales person does his or her just part then, his or her effort will be rewarded a hundred or perhaps a thousand fold. Through this fourth spiritual law of nature, a sales person may have a bad day in the field, or he or she may have an occasional, bad week but, he or she will NEVER have a bad month, once he or she put forth the just effort first. A sales person who truly understands the spiritual Law Of Compensation, is the one who you'll see attending all the prestigious company paid conventions and parties.

I should know, I was too, in sales profession for more than ten years. I have sold everything from selling products to businesses to selling insurance door-to-door. There were times when I would make 20 or 30 presentations daily and not one sale. I would get rejections after rejection on each call. I knew my product and new my rebuttals but, I just won't CLOSE any sale.

But, I'll tell you what? I won many President's club awards, went to many company fully paid trips. My recent was a 7-days fully paid air trip to El San Juan Resort in Puerto Rico. My office wall is loaded with trophies and outstanding achievement award certificates. I don't tell you all this to brag or to impress you. I tell all this because, I want to give you some proof of the validity of the soundness of the fourth law of nature COMPENSATION.

What I'm trying to say is that it is the 'intention' behind your own willingness to put forth the necessary efforts first in any undertaking, that is the most important thing. The rewards are always there but, the rewards are always directly proportional to the 'intensity' behind your efforts, the more you put forth your own efforts <u>first</u> in any undertaking, the more REWARDS, you'll receive in the end, through the spiritual law of Compensation. I have noticed with profound interest, just how people who are quite astute in business matters, use this fourth spiritual law of nature. These smart business people utilize this spiritual law of compensation by investing their own money <u>first</u> in, products, in advertising and promotions and other incentive and costly programs knowing that the spiritual law of compensation will take care of their justly deeds and efforts. And, they are more often than not, rewarded for all their hard work and investments.

IN IT'S HIGHEST FORM - THIS FOURTH SPIRITUAL LAW OF NATURE WORKS SOMETHING LIKE THIS:

"The good that we do for others, 'sets' into motion the good in GOD'S Mind, which RETURNS to us many times over in the good we receive from others". One of the most profound truth you'll learn when you practice this fourth spiritual law of nature is, that by applying this law of nature, you'll know THAT GOD IS AS MUCH "IN-US" AS GOD IS ALL ABOUT US. It is said, that nothing in this whole universe is 'static'. What I mean is that, our MIND and BODY and also the Universe are in 'constant' phase of what I call "Exchange". That is why, it is so important that we MUST 'give' or render a useful service FIRST, before we can expect to get or receive. "In every adversity there are seeds of equal opportunity". "In every seed there is a promise of thousands of forest. But, the SEED must NOT be 'hoarded'; it MUST be sowed, so that it can give it's intelligence to the fertile ground.

"When, as an example, the chronic poverty thinker, or a habitual negative thinker of many years, becomes the prosperity thinker — or an ardent positive thinker, we say that is a indeed a momentous 'Change' in the personality structure of the individual". "This 'Change', is the COMPENSATION of the individual's EFFORTS to HAVE A MIND THAT OPERATES EFFECTIVELY ON ALL LEVELS OF THE MIND". I hope you understand by now that I'm only trying to introduce the readers to that (OTHER-SELF) who, once it has been recognized will provide all the 'proof' anyone could ever desire or need. Which is only another way of saying that, I am endeavoring to introduce the readers to "Look Within" for all the answers to the riddle of life.

Truly, if all the world understood this fourth spiritual law of nature, and took full and complete possession of their own MINDS, and recognized their "Other-Self" (the self you don't see when you stand in front of a mirror) and looked-within for the answers — indeed, all the problem of the earth would be solved and peace, love, harmony and prosperity would be the experience of all human kind.

"They will be in flow of abundance by following the world's first COMPUTER-LIKE Flow Chart to reprogram their own MINDS for success using the Cutting-Edge Technology for success."

"They will be the ones to be the world's first to eliminate the seven major negative emotions from their MINDS for good, 'feed' the seven major positive emotions into their MINDS at all times and at all costs".

Moreover; they would learn, through the application of the fourth spiritual law of nature COMPENSATION the art of 'giving' and the science of 'receiving', and they would definitely 'keep' wealth and affluence — or — anything else they may want or need in life. Far, this is the second half of the PASSWORD of the 'Miracle' capable of making YOU FREE — TRULY FREE!

Finally, let me say this: I spend over twenty five years in research and studies in order to gather all the database for the manuscript of this book. Just think of it? Twenty five long years! Twenty five years without any direct financial compensation is an experience not calculated to give you sustained hope, I assure you. But, I knew from the beginning, that through that (power) of the fourth spiritual law Compensation, I will be rewarded a hundred or perhaps a thousand fold for every tiny effort I have put forth, when I finally do arrive. This much I know for sure.

In that, I have not been disappointed so far because, it has enabled me to earn my Doctoral Degree in the Science of Metaphysics. Recently, I was mentioned in the "Who's Who in Metaphysics", which is a most prestigious professional publication in the field of self-help and Metaphysics. I was the founder of an International Mind-Conditioning Society, an organization devoted exclusively to the teaching of this mind-power philosophy.

It will not surprise me one bit, if that (power) which gave the wisdom to write this manuscript, also make this one of the world's best selling books. I have seen it happened more than once. The reason I know that it could happen is that my major purpose in life is establish a scientific laboratory where people from all over the world come to 'connect' with each other and thus build a 'lasting' bond, relationships and rapport, and I believe this book may provide the missing 'link' to help fulfill my own 'mission statement' which is to, "To Advance Human Progress Through Preserving A FREE Mind!". WHAT MORE CAN ANYONE ASK FOR?

In closing, let me introduce a man whom I admire the most. His name is Dr. Deepak Chopra. He describes this spiritual law of nature in his mega best selling book, The Seven Spiritual Laws Of Success most eloquently, he says, and I quote, the more you give, the more you receive, because you'll 'keep' the abundance of the universe circulating in your life. "In fact anything that is of any value in life ONLY MULTIPLIES WHEN GIVEN". "That which does not multiply through giving is neither worth 'giving' nor worth 'receiving'. "If through the 'act' of giving, you feel you have lost something then, that gift is not truly 'giving' and will not cause increase."

Applying The Law Of Compensation!

I will put this law of Compensation into effect by making a commitment to take the following steps:

(1) I will take time each day to read at least two books on different religions, even I just read a paragraph or a chapter. I will read my own HOLY BOOK and perhaps THE HOLY QURAN. I will always keep an open mind to the truth found in any HOLY BOOK.

(2) I will make a commitment to myself to keep wealth circulating in my own life and the lives of all those I meet on a daily basis. I will practice the art of 'giving' and the science of 'receiving'. I will 'give' the life's most precious gifts: DESIRE, FAITH, LOVE, HOPE, CARING, ROMANCE and ENTHUSIASM.

(3) Wherever I go, And whoever I meet, I will silently say, "I LOVE YOU", This is a 'gift' I can give to everyone I come into contact with and this will start the process of circulating joy, wealth, affluence in my own life and the lives of others.

(4) I will share this whole book with one more person. I will help make this a better world in which to live. I will help build a lasting bond and rapport to 'connect' with others. I will help make America Strong and Wealthy — <u>ONE PERSON AT A TIME</u>!

Chapter 5
The Law Of Eternal Sorrow!!

"The sun and moon rotate in a predestined orbit. The plants and trees prostrate before him. He raised the heavens and set up everything in balance, so that you would maintain justice. So — maintain just measure and do not transgress against balance. He spread out the earth for the people. He is the Lord of East and West through all seasons. (Al-Rahman 55:2).

— THE HOLY QURAN —

The fifth spiritual law of nature is called the LAW OF ETERNAL SORROW!!

The basis of this law is that nature uses this spiritual law to 'communicate' with human beings. It's one of nature's clever device by which we are kept from becoming enslaved by complacency and self-satisfaction. In it's simplest form, the fifth spiritual law of nature, THE LAW OF ETERNAL SORROW, works something like this: "Nature forces us to take an introspective inventory of ourselves to search deeply into our hearts and into our souls for some answers to make life pay-off in terms of our own liking".

"Sorrow is a nature's clever device, through which it forces individuals to look deeply for the 'seeds' of opportunity in every adversity, every heart break, every pain, every suffering and disappointment." Through, SORROW, nature breaks up old 'habits' and replaces them with NEW and often much better 'habits'. Although, SORROW is NEVER invited by us, nevertheless; it is one of the more effective devices of nature to 'CONDITION' our MIND for success.

How can we apply this fifth spiritual law of ETERNAL SORROW, to our lives? If you want to enjoy the benefits of the LAW OF ETERNAL SORROW. If you want to make full use of the LAW OF ETERNAL SORROW, then you have to have access to it. One way to access the LAW OF ETERNAL SORROW is through understanding of 'energy' and bonding principle. In it's highest form, the fifth spiritual LAW OF NATURE works something like this:

"Everything in this universe is an 'energy'. The late, Albert Einstein, world's greatest mathematician and scholar proved this truth by his famous "theory-of-relativity". He proved that, "ALL MATTER IS ENERGY — AND ENERGY MATTER". Very simply stated: "Everything in this universe is 'connected' with each other through 'energy'. There is a greater power in the universe, And that (power) in the universe, COMMUNICATES only through 'energy' through everything. That (power) Communicates with all human beings only through the spiritual law of ETERNAL SORROW. Nature's intelligence (power) functions effortlessly, frictionlessly, spontaneously and when, we are in Harmony (second law) with nature, we as human too, communicate with this intelligence or 'energy' and BECOME ONE WITH EVERYTHING, AS EVERYTHING BECOMES ONE WITH US.

Now — how does all this work as far as the daily living of a person? Well, one sure fire way is to "think", of our own body (the self we see when we stand in front of a mirror) as DEVICE for controlling the 'energy'. It is a well established fact, that a human physical body can generate, store, and expand all 'energy'. If you know how to generate, store and expand this 'energy' in an efficient way, then you too can 'Create' any amount of wealth. All You have to do is learn how? When YOU are established in the knowledge of your true Self, you can make use of this nature's intelligence.

Let's sum up: There is a 'greater' power in this universe, and YOU too can use that (power) to 'mold' your own destiny here on earth. This is the very same (power) that communicates 'energy' and the life for the grass to grow (first law), fish to swim, birds to fly and flowers to bloom ...

When we 'struggle' against this universal 'intelligence' or that (power) we are actually struggling AGAINST the entire universe. Let me explain! "Our habits which do not conform to the over-all plan and purpose of this universe, are periodically broken-up through this vital fifth spiritual law of nature the ETERNAL SORROW." Nature leads man or woman through peace-ful means as long as man or woman co-operates but; she (nature) resorts to revolutionary methods, if man or woman rebels and 'neglects' or refuses to 'conform' to this spiritual law of nature.

After studying the case histories of several thousands of people, while putting this philosophy of personal-development together, I discovered with profound interest, that when a person comes to himself or herself and discovers that great (power) within his or her command, the revelation normally is due to a great SORROW or due to perhaps a failure in a business venture or due to some physical affliction BEYOND his or her own control. I will say 'amen' to that, because through my one and only great sorrow due to the failure in the business venture in the

Middle-East, I too, discovered the New way to my own soul, which gave me my personal FREEDOM, I would NEVER have known otherwise. And, this was this SORROW that actually led me, through the chain of events, toward this field of self-help, personal-development and Metaphysics and gave the opportunity to 'connect' with you, build a lasting bond and depart from this world as more EVOLVED soul.

Finally, I often thank my lucky star for having put through adversity, I would NEVER 'exchange' it with a million dollars. If it was not for this adversity, the manuscript of this book has never been written.

"It is true that I had suffered both physical pain and mental anguish, but I had not quit fighting; nor had I gone down under these circumstances. I had no financial means at that time, but I did have all the faculties of my own MIND, and I did intended to use those faculties, as the CREATOR intended I should."

"I had lost my business, my home, and my belongings, but so had thousands of other men and women, and I was no better than they. Many of my friends and associates and relatives declined to give me a helping hand when I most needed it, but their refusal injured them more than it did me, for it had deprived them of an opportunity to be merciful to a helpless person, and still left open a way by which I may regain my independence through the use of my own MIND".

"I do not regret the suffering I had gone through because it had given me the moral stamina with which I shall gain for myself FREEDOM in the future." "And, I do not hold any ill feelings against anyone for refusing to come to my rescue, because their neglect had provided me with a wonderful opportunity to comply with the fifth spiritual law of nature the ETERNAL SORROW."

During the adversities through which I had passed I had found the 'seed' of an equivalent benefit. It consisted in my discovery of that (power) of my own MIND and the means by which that (power) can be made the master of sorrow and suffering.

"Truly, in the hour of my greatest suffering I discovered my own soul, that invincible soul, the true Self."

But, the most wonderful benefit I had received from my adversities consisted in my discovery that SUFFERING (whether it be from physical pain or mental anguish), PLACES ONE IN A FAVORABLE POSITION FOR APPEAL TO THE CREATOR.

"I do not feel sorry for my self, but I do feel sorry for my own physical body, my own flesh and blood because they were not ready to embrace a wonderful opportunity to discover the greatness of the fifth spiritual law of nature. I also do feel sorry for all those people refusing to come to my rescue, because they were not ready to embrace this once in a life chance to discover the greatness of their own minds by exercise of mercy toward one who had the right to expect help from them".

"This adversity taught me a wonderful lesson and that is that our own true Self (God-Self) reveals ITSELF through 'silence' more readily than through the noises of our mad rush to accumulate material things". I am inclined to believe that (God-Self) that the total true Self; and everlasting peace-of-mind is available only to all those who properly INTERPRET and fully relate themselves to this particular fifth spiritual law of nature.

In all fairness, let me confess that the pay-off never would have come, this manuscript never would have been written and this philosophy of individual achievement never would have been organized, had I not learned the 'blessed' art of "TRANSMUTING" unpleasant circumstances into construction ACTION. That is why, it so important for you to put these laws of nature into effect by making a commitment to <u>take the steps</u> mentioned at the end of each chapter.

REMEMBER ALWAYS THIS WORD: "TRANSMUTE"!

"If you should ever feel that your own SORROWS are much greater than you can ever bear then, just keep your own mind so busily engaged in thinking of something constructive that no time is left for you to feel any sorrow".

"And, when sorrow over-takes you, follow the same plan by turning your dominating 'thoughts' toward the attainment of some as yet un-attained purpose or goal in life that (literally) no time is left for self-pity and then, devise means and plans and ways of attaining that aim or goal in life. DO THIS AND YOU WILL SURELY DISCOVER A HIDDEN "<u>ASSET</u>" YOU DID NOT KNOW YOU POSSESS!!

In closing, the 'essence' of the fifth spiritual law of nature is this:

"YOU GOT TO GET THROUGH THE NEGATIVES TO GO THROUGH THE POSITIVES" What it means is simply this, that he who achieves little, sacrifices little, and he who achieves much MUST sacrifice much. The bigger the aim or purpose in life, the bigger the sorrows far, this is the law.

Applying The Law Of Eternal Sorrow!!

I will put this law of ETERNAL SORROW into effect by making a commitment to take the following steps:

(1) I will share this whole book with one more person, whether it be my spouse, my children, my friend or an associate. I will give this book as gift so that it will help me to do my part to make my own community a better place in which to live.

(2) I will talk about this book with every one I will meet today. I know that the word-of-mouth, is the best way to pass on any good information. I'll do my part to help 'connect' with other human beings with similar interests and thus build a lasting bond and relationships world wide.

(3) I will make a commitment to myself to keep wealth and abundance circulating in my own life and the lives of people world wide by eliminating the seven major negative emotions from my MIND. FEAR, HATE, JEALOUSY, SUPERSTITION, GREED, REVENGE AND ANGER. These are the seven major enemies of mankind.

(4) I will help keep the "MISSION" alive by sharing these laws of nature wherever I go, and whoever I meet during the day as I go about my business. I will support the "Mission" statement: "TO ADVANCE HUMAN PROGRESS BY PRESERVING A FREE MIND"

Chapter 6
The Law Of Eternal Struggle!!

"Whoever has done an atom's weight of good, will see it and whoever has done an atom's weight of evil, will also see it." (Al-Zilzal 99:2).
— THE HOLY QURAN —

The sixth spiritual law of nature is called the LAW OF ETERNAL STRUGGLE!

The basis for this sixth spiritual law of nature is that so called STRUGGLES, is a nature's clever device through it forces all individuals to PROGRESS and EXPAND and become STRONG through resistance. Through this sixth spiritual law of nature, everything in this whole wide universe must go through struggles. Let me EXPLAIN! "Ever notice, that the strongest trees are not those in heavily protected forests but, the trees which stand in open space where they are in constant STRUGGLE with wind and other elements of weather".

The same way, all individuals MUST experience STRUGGLES and undergo hardships in order to become strong.

Through this sixth spiritual law of nature, we human beings, 'accept' all those so called 'struggles' as mere circumstances of opportunities through which we may prepare ourselves for still greater and better plans of existence than the one on which we now dwell. It is said, that 'struggles' are often just a 'test' from our CREATOR to see, who will have the 'guts' to get-up and make a fresh start.

In doing my research and studies for putting this sixth spiritual law of nature, I had noticed with profound interest, that NO MAN OR WOMAN IN THE HISTORY OF MAN-KIND, WAS EVER CHOSEN AS A LEADER WHO HAD NOT BEEN FIRST THOROUGHLY TESTED BY THE SIXTH SPIRITUAL LAW OF ETERNAL STRUGGLE!

"Struggles become either a curse or a blessing for the individuals depending upon just "How" it is taken." By utilizing this sixth spiritual law of nature, we 'accept' that all those so called 'struggles' in our own lives are but, a TRANSITIONAL stage leading to greater good and abundance in our own lives.

How can we apply this sixth spiritual law of ETERNAL STRUGGLE, to our lives? If you want to enjoy the benefits of the LAW OF ETERNAL STRUGGLE. If you want to make full use of the LAW OF ETERNAL STRUGGLE, then you have to have access to it. One way to access the LAW OF ETERNAL STRUGGLE is through understanding the principle of self-preservation. Let me explain!

"Everything in this whole universe must go through 'struggles' in order to PROGRESS and expand and become strong through resistance. Birds struggle to find food for themselves and for their off springs. They struggle to find shelters during rain, wind and all the other elements of weather. Flowers, plants and trees are in constant struggle in the forest to seek food and water. Weaker creatures are in constant struggle for individual survival from the stronger creatures.

Struggles are not just limited to animals and human beings, they also break up old over-all plans for this universe either by world wars, floods, earth quakes, epidemics of disease, and forces the universe to start all over again.

In it's simplest form, the sixth spiritual law of nature works something like this:

Through this sixth spiritual law of nature the ETERNAL STRUGGLE, we, 'accept' all so called struggles as mere circumstances of opportunities through which we may prepare ourselves for still greater and better plans of existence that the one on which we now dwell.

After studying the case histories of countless thousands of people in all walks of life during the last twenty five years, I discovered that no man or woman ever achieved riches, whether it be of material possessions of a lasting inner peace, who had not been thoroughly tested by the law of ETERNAL STRUGGLE.

Almost every person in this whole wide world who achieved riches of both money or spirit in a big way, admitted that once he and she was so down in his or her personal, professional, and spiritual life, and the turning-point was this sixth law of ETERNAL STRUGGLE. It seems as though, the law of ETERNAL STRUGGLE somehow, forces you to the point where you feel there seem to be no reason to continue, everything will tell you to give up and quit trying, some even go to the point of ending the life, it is at this point, and peak of your depression when you usually begin to find the answers one-by-one to the riddle of life, and more often than not make a new and better start in life.

I will say 'amen' to that because due to the failure in the business venture in the Middle-East, I, too was forced to either end the life or look for and make a new and better start.

I was forced to STRUGGLE for twenty five years, to maintain myself economically while doing the necessary research for organizing these seven spiritual laws of nature.

Twenty five years of hard work and struggles, without ANY direct financial compensation is an experience not calculated to give one sustained hope. I assure you! But, this was the price I had to pay for the privilege of putting the world's first COMPUTER-LIKE Flow Chart to reprogram the MIND for success using a NEW Cutting-Edge Technology for success by eliminating the seven major negative emotions from the MIND for good, and by feeding the seven major positive emotions into the MIND, at all times and at all costs.

If this self-knowledge is able to transform your own life, no matter how small, then my twenty five years of sorrows as well all struggles will have been well rewarded, and I do thank you from the bottom of my heart.

I must confess, that I have not been totally disappointed, but I have been overwhelmed with the bountiful manner in which this sixth spiritual law of ETERNAL STRUGGLE has responded and paid me tribute for the past twenty five years of struggles that went into my work.

And, it was this STRUGGLE in preparing myself with the necessary knowledge to produce this world's first Computer-Like Flow Chart to reprogram the MIND, that actually led me through the chain of events to my own "MISSION" in life. It was the self-knowledge that taught me that I have a special and unique "talent", and I was to give this self-knowledge to others and not just keep it for myself. It was this self-knowledge that taught me that my "talent" is so unique that ONLY I could do better than anyone else in this whole wide world, and there is a need for my special and unique "talent", what greater rewards can a person ask for?

I found my own "MISSION" in life by answering the two most important questions. (1) What Do I want in life? (2) Where Am I going? Answer these two questions truthfully and you'll have given your life a new purpose and direction. But, perhaps, more importantly, these two questions will surely lead you to your own "MISSION" or purpose in life, just as they did for thousands of others who took the time to answer these two vital questions.

The answers to these two questions will reveal some amazing things. So — please do some soul-searching or deep-probing while thinking about these two questions, they will surely pay you much dividends. The answers to these question will reveal among other things, that there is definite need for your special and unique "Talent", and when you match this need with the creative expression of your unique "talent" that's when you begin to 'access' to infinite, unbounded creativity. Furthermore; expressing your special and unique "talent" to fulfill your own needs, could very well create an unlimited wealth and abundance for life. All you have to do is to capitalize on your own inherent God-given special and unique "talent". When you blend your unique and special "talent" with service to others, that is when you experience your true Self the (Other-Self).

Just remember this: That you have a "mission" in your life for which only you were chosen to fulfill it. Your own mission mainly deals with service to humanity — and — to serve other fellow human-beings.

THE WHOLE PURPOSE OF THE SIXTH SPIRITUAL LAW OF ETERNAL STRUGGLE IS TO HELP YOU FIND YOUR OWN MISSION IN LIFE AND FULFILL IT.

Applying The Law Of Eternal Struggle

I will put this law of ETERNAL STRUGGLE into effect by making a commitment to take the following steps:

(1) I will make a list of my unique talents. Then I will list all the things that I love to do while expressing my special and unique talents. When I express my unique talents and use them in the service to humanity that is when I will create wealth and abundance in my life as well as the lives of all those I encounter.

(2) I will ask myself daily, "What do I want in life?" "Where am I going?" "How can I serve other fellow human beings?" "What is my own mission in life?" "How can I express my special and unique talent to fulfill my own needs?" "How can I have access to infinite, unbounded creativity."

(3) I will do some soul-searching or deep-probing while thinking about the above questions. The answers to the above questions will allow me to help and serve my fellow human beings. I will often ask myself daily, "How can I help?" This will help me to serve others with love.

(4) I will remind myself to practice each and every step as mentioned at the end of every chapter.

Chapter 7
The Law Of Eternal Change

"He is the only God. God is absolute. He neither begets nor He begotten. There is no one equal to Him. (Al-Ekhlas 112:2).

— THE HOLY QURAN —

The seventh spiritual law of nature is called the LAW OF ETERNAL CHANGE!

The basis of this seventh spiritual law is that, so called CHANGES in our own lives is a nature's clever 'tool' for human progress. Eternal Change is a spiritual law of nature without which, there could be no such thing as civilization. Circumstances of life which CHANGE may just be a part of our CREATOR (GOD) and his over-all plan in connection with human destiny. It is said, that a CHANGE is often, just a test from our CREATOR to see who will have the insight to 'accept' a new direction in life.

Although the seventh spiritual law of nature is The Eternal Change, it could also be called The Eternal Struggle, because they are the principles that nature uses to create everything in material existence — every this that we see, hear, smell, taste and touch. Through the spiritual laws of CHANGE and STRUGGLE, all individuals acquire flexibility of personality and the capacity to ADAPT themselves to all circumstances of life which affect them.

Our habits which do not conform to the over-all plan and purpose of this universe are periodically broken up, either by world wars, floods, epidemics of disease, and are forced to start all over again.

Nature lead human beings through CHANGE or STRUGGLE by peace-full means as long they co-operate but, nature resorts to revolutionary methods, if human beings rebel and neglect, or refuse to conform to these two spiritual laws of nature. Remember this and profit by it the next time you meet face-to-face with CHANGE OR STRUGGLE.

And, instead of crying out in rebellion, or SHIVERING with fear, HOLD your 'head' high, and LOOK in all direction for the 'seed' of an equivalent benefit in every circumstance of CHANGE or STRUGGLE.

We can apply the spiritual law of ETERNAL CHANGE the same way we learned to use the spiritual law of ETERNAL STRUGGLE.

In it's simplest form the seventh spiritual law of nature works something like this:

"Everything in this universe MUST go through CHANGE! Why? Because it's the LAW.

Through this spiritual law of ETERNAL CHANGE, day changes into night, sun changes into moon, summer with winter, matter changes into 'energy' — and 'energy' changes into matter. A seed of an acorn changes into an oak tree. A seed of a flower blossom and changes beautiful tree. A child changes into an adult. The point is that the only thing constant in this universe is a CHANGE.

Now — how does all this work as far as daily living of a person?

Well, all habits and 'thoughts' and emotions are continuously reshaping themselves into a SYSTEM of human relationships leading toward greater harmony and better understanding among each other. The fear, the failure, the shocks and disappointments in human relations are all designed to shake us loose from habits to which we so tenaciously cling, so we may adopt better ones.

In it's highest form, this spiritual law of ETERNAL CHANGE goes something like this:

"To acquire anything in this physical world, you have to relinquish your attachment to it first." By relinquishing your own attachment to anything in the physical universe, does not necessarily mean that you give up your desire or the intention to create your desire. You don't give up the intention, and you don't give up your desire. YOU ONLY GIVE UP YOUR ATTACHMENT TO RESULT.

"The moment you relinquish your attachment to the result, combining one-pointed attention with detachment at the same time. You will that which you desire anything you want can be acquired through detachment, because detachment is based on the unquestioning belief in that (power) of your true self.

The whole purpose of the seventh spiritual law of nature is to help you 'experience' of being ONE within Oneself. This 'experience' can only be described as an 'experience' in which one discovers that they are ultimately ONE WITH ALL THINGS AS ALL THINGS ARE ONE WITH THEM.

This universal ONENESS within ONE-SELF may last only a few seconds when 'experienced' as a MIND expansion 'experience' — but, it's effect, even if 'experienced' only once in a person's life time remains the major influence or criteria of 'identity-structure' in the individual. All those who have 'experienced' it INTUITIVELY do agree with me that it is an experience where as one has become one with stars, nature, all living things and the nature. I have personally 'experienced' this universal ONENESS within One-Self for the last twenty five years.

Applying The Law Of Eternal Change!!

I will put this law of ETERNAL CHANGE INTO EFFECT by making a commitment to take the following steps:

(1) I will make a list of the seven major negative emotions and consciously try to eliminate them from my own mind for good.

(2) I will make a list of the seven major positive emotions and consciously try to feed into my own mind at all times and at all costs.

(3) I will reprogram my own MIND using the <u>COMPUTER-LIKE</u> Flow Chart, using Cutting-Edge Technology for success.

(4) I will take full and complete possession of my own MIND simply by CONTROLLING my own thinking.

(5) I will accept each day as it is. I will accept person as he or she is — and not as he or she should be. I will welcome all new changes that occur during the day.

(6) I will remind myself that all struggles and changes in my life are for my own good. I will accept all changes with open mind and look for the 'seed' of a benefit in each change.

(7) I will thank GOD for the understanding of the seven spiritual LAWS OF NATURE and thus enabling me to understand myself.

Chapter 8
You're In The Flow Of Abundance!!

"I want to know God's thought ... the rest are details.

— Albert Einstein

Do you want what you want? I mean, do you 'really' and truly want prosperity, success, happiness, and abundance in your life? Do you 'really' want respect, praise, more time, and more freedom? Are you ready to be FREE ... truly free, with the personal freedom that comes ONLY by unleashing your Mind from the bondage of all self-imposed limitations? Do you want to enjoy the benefits of the seven spiritual laws of nature? Do you want to make full use of the creativity which in inherent in the seven spiritual laws of nature? Do you want to tune-in to the Mind of Nature? Do you want to 'access' it's infinite, unbounded creativity? Do you want to harness that (power) which runs and control this universe with a perfect 'system' and plan? Do you want to use the 'master' key to all riches wisely? Do you want to know your "Other-Self" the "GOD-SELF"?

Then my friend, all you have to do is get in the flow!

This chapter will take you there. It's based on a simple concept: "When you direct your own MIND, you automatically direct your own emotions"

"And, when you direct your own emotions appropriately, your own 'behavior' will bring about the results you desire."

Direct your own MIND and Emotions (both negative and positive) and they will surely put YOU into the 'Flow' of abundance, and make you FREE of all self-imposed limitations, give you an access to the infinite, unbounded creativity of the Mind of nature.

And, I believe that the Mind-Conditioning Flow Chart is the only way to guide you step-by-step toward your destination (on page 63). YOU'LL FIND A SAMPLE FLOW CHART LIKE THE ONES COMPUTER PROGRAMMERS MIGHT USE.

Later, we'll plug the necessary data (information) into the flow chart and see how a computer would accomplish our Mind-Conditioning or mind-programming task for us. But, for now all you need to know is that a SQUARE REPRESENTS A COMMAND, and a DIAMOND REPRESENTS A QUESTION, and an ARROW INDICATES THE FLOW OF DATA (information).

Frankly, my own knowledge of computer programming is pitifully limited. But, I do know computers work on two fundamental principles: a command, followed by a question. I also know that computer programming is nothing more nor less than a method by which one communicates with the computer. In other words, it's a language the computer understands.

Before a computer can help you solve a problem or aid you in any other way, you must speak it's language or it will nor heed your call. To speak a computer's language, we use flow chart. And, that is purpose of the flow chart. THAT'S ALL YOU NEED TO KNOW ABOUT COMPUTER PROGRAMMING: A Square Represents a Command, A Diamond represents a Question and an Arrow indicates the Flow Of Data.

Now — if you are wondering what all this have to do with The Mind-Conditioning, then let me assure right at the start, that the reason why it's so important to FOLLOW this flow chart is that by a method somewhat similar to the one used for computer programming for finding solutions to all problems, you can the same way, PROGRAM or "CONDITION" your own MIND to lead you on to every imaginable achievements as easily as your comb your hair or eat your food when hungry.

IT WILL NOT SURPRISE ME ONE BIT, IF SOMEONE, SOMEWHERE, SOMEHOW COMES UP WITH AN ACTUAL MIND-CONDITIONING PROGRAM (like the floppy disk, software) that you can use on the computer to reprogram your own mind but, for now, just remember that I pioneered the concept.

So — the 'key' that unlocks the door to all the fortunes of your own MIND is none other than YOUR own ability to "CONDITION" or Program your own MIND to access the mind of nature and make full use of the infinite, unbounded creativity inherent in all the laws of nature. And, that's where the world's first flow chart to program or condition your mind will play a big role.

I believe, that the only known method of 'conditioning' or programming your own MIND to be prepared to 'access' to receive all the fortunes from the mind is by taking full and complete control of your own thinking and emotions (both negative and positive) and the easiest way to control our own 'thoughts' and emotions is <u>COMPUTER-LIKE</u> Flow Chart. (using as a step-by-step guide).

It has taken me twenty five years of mind-conditioning practices to finally produce a flow chart to reprogram the mind for success and I can honestly say that my own mind is under my full control about 99% of the time.

Being human, I still lose control once in a while but, I know that I can always get in the flow and take the control.

The whole purpose of using the COMPUTER-LIKE flow chart is that once your own MIND is properly programmed, you'll be in the possession of a MASTER-KEY that will allow you to be aware of certain things: The very first thing it will do for you is that you are suddenly aware that you have that (power) to take full and complete possession of your own MIND by controlling EVERY thought that enters into the MIND and thus, the MASTER-KEY will help you direct your MIND toward your own personal goals, desires and aspirations.

The second thing this intangible MASTER-KEY will do for you is that it will help you suddenly become 'conscious' of the COINCIDENCES or of what is commonly known as "CHANCE" happenings in your life. Let me explain!

Have you ever had a hunch, or an intuition concerning something you wanted to do? And, after you had half forgotten about it and focused on other things, you suddenly met someone or read something or went somewhere that actually, led to the very same opportunity you envisioned?

Remember this: "Nothing in your own life happens to just be an accident, it is all planned for you. The daily coincidences in your own life are not mere just coincidences, they are brought to your attention to complete a picture, or give you a missing link for some as yet accomplished goal, desire or aspiration.

I always consciously 'watch' for those so called, coincidences on a daily basis and religiously follow EACH AND EVERY 'coincidence' I encounter, and always over-ride my own logic or reasoning no matter sound and logical it may appear to be at the moment. The MASTER-KEY is intangible but, it's the most powerful 'tool' you have for Mind reprogramming.

Finally, let us sum up!

Directing your own MIND and EMOTIONS (both negative & positive), puts YOU into the flow of abundance, making you free and giving you 'access' to the life's bountiful riches of both money and the spiritual.

I believe, that this is the world's FIRST, <u>COMPUTER-LIKE</u> Flow Chart that will enable you to reprogram your MIND for success using the Cutting-Edge Technology for success, happiness and peace and prosperity. You'll not find it anywhere and it's not available through any book store. It's available only through this book.

This flow chart is based on the fact that the MIND can be re-programmed for success just as the computer is programmed for solving a particular problem. As you may notice, that the Flow Chart is very similar to the ones professional programmers might use to solve a problem. At first glance, the Flow Chart may seem complicated. But, it really isn't. It's a simple 'tool' or 'blue-print', if you will, that graphically represents The Mind-Conditioning or Mind-Programming Process! The process of finding the MASTER-KEY that unlocks the door to the abundance of riches and fortunes is NOT difficult once you know how?

IT ALL STARTS BY PROGRAMMING YOUR OWN MIND USING THE WORLD'S FIRST FLOW CHART!

"If you are familiar with computer programming then; you of course, know that it consists of a set of instructions or 'steps' that tell the computer exactly how to handle and solve a specific problem. And, to plan the 'process' from asking the question to the delivery of the results require that you EXTRACT CERTAIN UN-DESIRABLE DATA (information) FROM THE COMPUTER AND "FEED" CERTAIN DESIRABLE DATA INTO THE COMPUTER.

In other words; you are 'speaking' (so to speak) with the computer in it's own language and THAT'S WHAT IS COMMONLY KNOWN AS IN THE COMPUTER WORLD, AS COMPUTER PROGRAMMING.

So — let's get to it!

Let's discuss exactly how to program the MIND by recognizing and by eliminating some of the Mind's most powerful adversaries. Then, you too can CONDITION or program your own MIND to attract all riches and fortunes.

For now, just look at the page 63, and start to imagine yourself in the powerful "FLOW" of The Mind-Conditioning Process.

When you're in that flow (soon now!), you'll begin to experience freedom, peace of mind, and fulfillment of your desires.

Get ready, because you'll be AMAZED at how simple it is to reprogram your own MIND.

Are you ready? I thought so ...

A SAMPLE FLOW-CHART

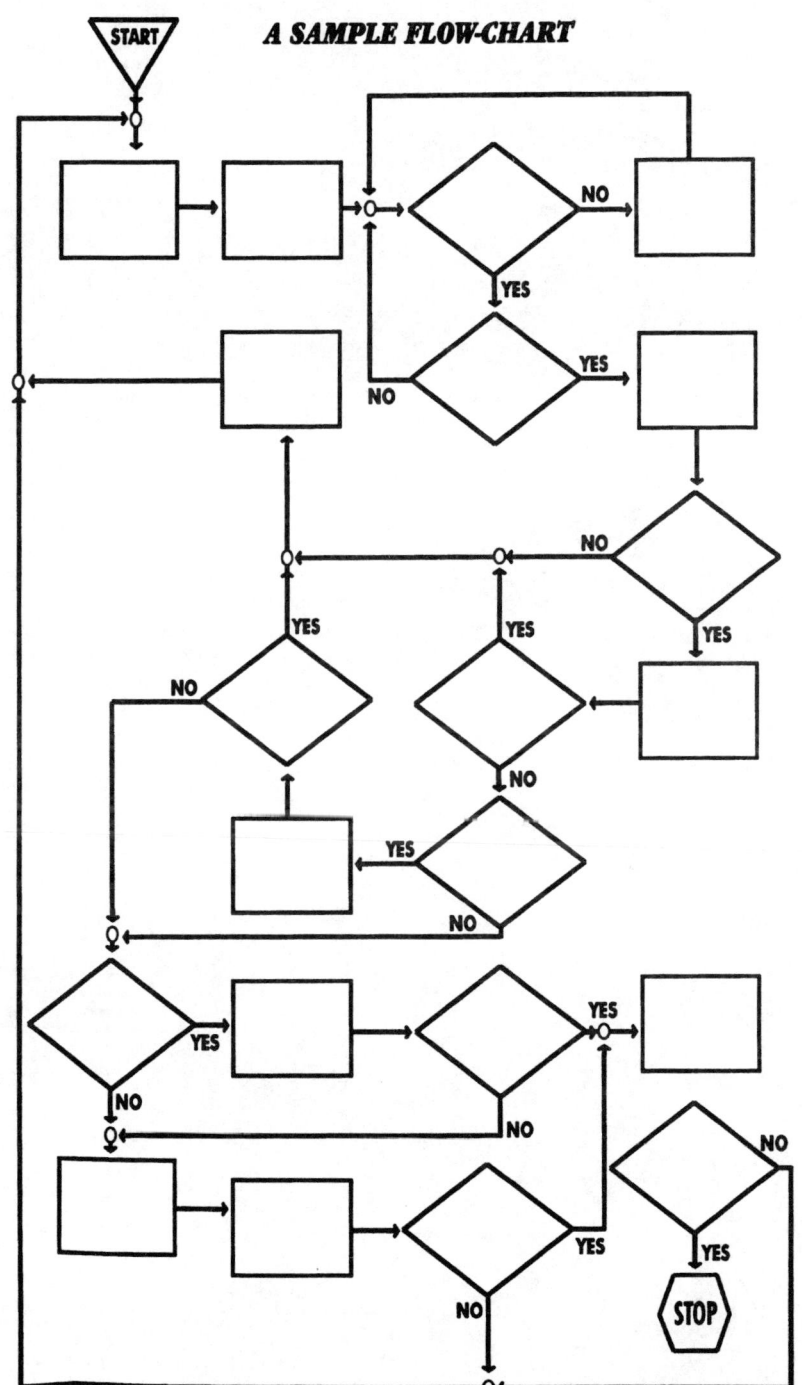

Chapter 9
Unlock The Door To A Gold-Mine Of Riches

"More gold is hidden in your own-mind than any gold-mine".

— Mushtaq Jaafri

By now you're no doubt ready to start reaping the rewards of more money, more time, more enjoyment from life, more personal freedom ... in short, more of everything you desire. ALL IT TAKES IS THE MASTER KEY TO ALL RICHES. With it you can unlock the door of your MIND, where you'll find unlimited abundance, tremendous freedom, and total peace of mind. The Master-Key, of course is The Mind-Conditioning System and it's Flow Chart Concept. This Master-Key gives YOU 'access' to all the riches in the gold-mine of your own-mind. This chapter shows you how to begin The mind programming process, and use the Master-Key to CONDITION your own-mind for prosperity on all levels. As I mentioned before, the flow chart we are talking about here is very similar to the kinds used by computer programmers. If you are familiar with computer programming, then you know it is based on a 'set' of instructions or 'steps' that tell the computer exactly how to handle and solve a problem. The process of computer programming starts with a question and ends with the delivery of the results. It requires the programmer to 'eliminate' or extract certain undesirable information and to 'feed' or force certain desirable information into the computer. All the while, the programmer speaks with computer in it's own language. THIS IS THE NUTS AND BOLTS OF COMPUTER PROGRAMMING!

So — what does computer programming have to do with mind-conditioning? Well, just as computers can be programmed to solve problems, you can condition your Mind to find the riches and fortunes available to all humans. In much the same way a computer is programmed, you can condition your own MIND by eliminating negative information, and by feeding it certain desirable information, and BY SPEAKING TO THE MIND, IT'S OWN LANGUAGE. By so doing, your own mind will be conditioned to reduce the solutions of your problems into a form that can be recognized. The form may be a hunch, a thought, an idea, an inspiration, or guidance, or just about anything else.

Now — what are the negative bits of information you need to eliminate from your own mind? They're what I've called in the mind programming 'The 7- Major Negative Emotions!'

As we've discussed, in order to condition your own mind you do need to 'speak' to the Mind in it's own language. Otherwise; it will not heed you call. That language is THE LANGUAGE OF EMOTIONS, feelings, beliefs, hope and faith, The Mind understands the language of EMOTIONS ONLY. This is the language our Mind understands best. When that language is filled with negativity, and with all the seven major negative emotions, what effect do you think it has on your Mind? Doesn't it slow down your progress in life and keep you away from your goals or desires or aims or aspirations? Doesn't it limit life and make it harder - if not impossible for you to prosper? Of course. That's why it's absolutely essential to completely 'eliminate' the 7-major negative Emotions if you are to condition your Mind and 'dig-up' the gold that awaits for you there. If you want your own life to 'really' take off, YOU MUST MAKE A CLEAN SWEEP OF THE 7-MAJOR EMOTIONS FOR GOOD!

I can't stress this point strong enough:
"IF YOU WANT TO "DIG-UP" THE GOLD IN THE GOLD-MINE OF YOUR OWN-MIND, ALL 7-MAJOR NEGATIVE EMOTIONS MUST BE COMPLETELY ELIMINATED FROM YOUR OWN-MIND FOR GOOD".

You see, the presence of even one negative Emotion can eliminate the chance of ever conditioning the Mind. When that happens, the things you desire in life will remain beyond your grasp.

That's why I call these 7-Major negative Emotions my own powerful enemies, and I treat them as such. It took me 25 years of hard work to completely eliminate these seven major enemies from my own Mind for good. Fortunately, you'll be able to do the same in much less time. It took me so long because no one had blazed this trail before me, so I didn't know just what I was up against. When I did figure out that I was up against 7-Major Emotions, it took more time to figure out how to defeat them. To save you all the time it took me to work this out, I'll surely lead you to these 7-Major enemies of humankind, introduce them to you, help you meet them courageously, and finally show you just how to 'get rid' of them one-by-one, and for good. By the way, as you'll soon see, this is where the <u>COMPUTER-LIKE</u> Flow Chart Concept comes into action.

It took me 25 years of hard work to 'devise' this unique Mind-Conditioning or Mind-Programming

System. But, all you have to do is to follow the <u>COMPUTER-LIKE</u> Flow Chart. But, for now, let me introduce you to the seven enemies of mankind. They're what I call them the 7-Major Negative Emotions. The 7-Major Negative Emotions are ranked in order of severity, and this very FIRST one certainly qualifies as the MOST 'severe' and potentially disabling.

Seven Major Enemies Of Mankind!

FEAR

The very first negative EMOTION of the list of 7-Major Emotions, in the order of their severity is none other than the EMOTION OF FEAR! Yes — FEAR, does head the list of seven major negative emotions that MUST ELIMINATE COMPLETELY FROM YOUR OWN MIND FOR GOOD. The reason why FEAR has been placed at the 'head' of the list is that Fear is one of the most difficult of all 7-major negative emotions. It is the MOST difficult to master, although; not impossible. This enemy without a doubt THE most destructive of all 7-Major emotions, and it's absolutely essential that you eliminate FEAR from your own MIND completely for good.

One thing I've learned during my 25 years research and studies, is that before we can master an enemy, we must know it's name, it's HABITS, and it's place of ABODE. So — to begin with, you must know that there are many names by which this powerful foe, and enemy is called, but the most common 'names' are: The Fear of Illness, The Fear of Poverty and The Fear Of Criticism.

It is said that, at the bottom of most of our worries, doubts, indecision, anxieties, frustrations and heartbreaks are always these three (fears) enemies! And, then slightly less common 'names' of this human enemy number one are: The Fear Of Death, The Fear Of Loss of Love and The Fear Of Old Age. These are the basic six enemies of all humankind. If you don't experience any of these six basic fears, count yourself fortunate, However; I'll bet you a penny, that chances are good that you too (like myself) have experienced at least one or more of them at some time.

When this enemy (Fear) comes into your own life, it usually appears in a different form and from different direction than you generally expect. That is one of the 'tricks' of FEAR, perhaps that's why so many people fail to recognize FEAR, because it has a 'sly' habit of slipping in the back door, and often it comes disguised in the form of 'misfortune', such as a death of a loved one, temporary defeat, or a failure in a business venture. This enemy dwells in your own MIND, and it's nothing more than a 'State-Of-Mind' but, it is sufficient to destroy one's chance of 'finding' the "MasterKey" to the doors that open to all your riches and fortunes. The majority of people if asked, what they FEAR most, would reply that "I FEAR NOTHING". This reply, of course; would be inaccurate because most people do not realize that they are bound, 'conditioned' and wiped both spiritually and physically through some form of FEAR. There is no way that you could possibly have a positive 'state-of-mind' (the very first step toward programming the Mind), without completely ELIMINATING this MOST powerful foe and enemy from your Mind for good.

Now — there certain FEARS that are valid, and should remain in your Mind. For example, the fear of drowning, if you don't happen to know how to swim. Or, the FEAR of a snake, if you happen to see a snake marching toward you (although, I know of people who permit rattle snakes to bite and live). I have also seen with my own two eyes, people who walk on burning fire with naked feet without any harm or fear whatsoever.

But, when we talk about Mind-Conditioning, we're NOT talking about protective fears. Instead, we're referring to those fears that are the 'enemies' of a healthy mental attitude... the FEARS that hinder human progress in a hundred different ways.

HATE

Hate is number two among the 7-major negative emotions, and this should be your second major negative emotion (enemy) to eliminate from your own mind toward the process of programming the MIND for finding the FREE gold from the gold-mine of your own-mind!

Hate is second only to FEAR when it comes to the severity level of the 7-major negative emotions. Elimination of all HATE from your life is a major step toward finding the "Master-Key" to all riches. (The first step is the elimination of fear). Know This enemy number two well, because HATE paralyzes the faculties of reason, and kills self-reliance. It takes the charm out of one's personality and destroys the possibility of clear thinking. This enemy number two kills LOVE, FAITH, HOPE, DESIRE, ROMANCE, ENTHUSIASM and assassinates the finer (POSITIVE) emotions of the heart. It discourages friendships and invites disaster in a hundred different forms. If you truly want to program your own-mind to bring you all the fortune and success from the gold-mine of your own-mind, then you MUST try to eliminate HATE from your own-mind for good.

JEALOUSY

Your enemy number three, as far as your healthy mental attitude is concerned, is none other than, you guessed it, "JEALOUSY!" Eliminating JEALOUSY from your own MIND is the third step in programming the MIND for total freedom, peace and prosperity. (The first and second steps are the elimination of FEAR and HATE).

JEALOUSY discourages initiative and leads to uncertainty of purpose in life. It wipes out enthusiasm and makes self-control an impossibility. Nothing will bring so much suffering and humility than Jealousy. Only those who have truly experienced this powerful enemy (Jealousy) understand the full meaning of this most miserable foe. Get-rid of this merciless enemy from your own mind for good, and remember this always: If you truly want to PROGRAM your own mind, and if you sincerely desire to accumulate riches or fortunes, whether measured in terms of money, or a 'state-of-mind' of far greater value than money, you MUST eliminate this enemy known as Jealousy from your own-mind.

SUPERSTITION

The fourth major enemy of all human achievement is Superstition! Just think what modern civilization would be like if we had allowed this negative emotion to dominate our Minds. If superstitious people had their way, we probably would not have many of our modern day miraculous advantages of life, such as airplanes and telephones.

After all, most average people of that day were extremely suspicious of the notion that machines could fly, and they certainly did not believe it would be possible to 'hear' someone's voice from thousands of miles away. And remember how many people were sure that SPACE exploration would bring down all kinds of disasters on humankind, or perhaps the end of the world?

GREED

Your fifth enemy, that eventually destroys your positive mental attitude is none other than Greed!

(FEAR, HATE, JEALOUSY and SUPERSTITION are first four enemies).

Getting-rid of GREED from your own mind for good is the fifth step in the programming of your own MIND. It's quite interesting to note that originally, the negative EMOTION of Greed, grew mostly out of our inherent tendency to 'prey' upon our fellow human beings economically. You see, nearly all nonhuman (animals) are motivated by an instinct alone; and their capacity to think is very limited, therefore, they 'prey' upon one another PHYSICALLY only.

We humans, on the other hand, have intuition and the ability to think and reason. So, we do not eat fellow human beings bodily but, we get more satisfaction out of eating financially. So eager is our ambition to possess wealth and out do others that we will acquire it whatever manner we can, through legal methods if possible, and through other methods if necessary or expedient. People who have properly programmed their minds do not long for anything they have not acquired justly. They do not hold on to material possessions for dear life; instead, they share what they have (both tangible or intangible) with others.

REMEMBER THIS, TOO: The blessings we share with others multiply and stay with us. The blessings we keep just for ourselves diminish in the long run, far; this is the essence of the Mind Programming.

REVENGE

The sixth enemy of all humankind is called the Revenge! Although; it's the weakest of all the other five enemies, nevertheless; it is also considered a ruthless enemy, because it destroys ambition, beclouds the memory, and invites failure in every conceivable form. It kills LOVE, and discourages friendship, and leads to sleepless nights and miserable, unhappy days. All those who have suffered this ruthless enemy, know exactly what I'm talking about. Revenge destroys the faculty of imagination and turns willpower into nothingness and like GREED, can ruin your own life.

ANGER

The last enemy of all human achievements is known as "ANGER"! And, it's the seventh and final step toward programming your own MIND for prosperity. Get this childish enemy out of your hair and out of your <u>MIND</u>! Then, you'll be well on your way to possess a Mind that is <u>totally positive</u>. But, let me be perfectly frank with you. This is a childish enemy that is one of the meanest child of all enemies of human-beings because it diverts your concentration and efforts, robs your initiative, and restricts your individuality. Anger is usually expressed by finding faults with others, and by the HABIT of looking for the negative side of every circumstances. The person who expresses 'anger' through his or her words is almost certain to experience the results of those words in the form of a destructive 'Kick-Back'.

A person with a "Conditioned' or "PROGRAMMED" Mind develops the HABIT of controlling this childish enemy (ANGER), as well the other six major negative emotions.

THERE YOU HAVE THEM, ALL OF THE KNOWN SEVEN MAJOR NEGATIVE EMOTIONS!!!!!

Having read the seven major negative emotions, you may have observed that while meeting with these seven major enemies face-to-face, you were probably 'lifted' to a higher level of mental stimulation. That's splendid! (You are on the right track, if you did.)

Our next logical step in the process of Mind-Conditioning or Mind Programming, is to 'plug-in' all this data, this information and into the <u>COMPUTER-LIKE</u> Flow Chart, and see just how, we will use the Flow Chart using the Cutting-Edge Technology to PROGRAM or CONDITION our own MIND just as a computer programmer will use to accomplish any task of solving a problem.

BE SURE TO ACT ON THE NEXT CHAPTER OF THIS REMARKABLE NEW BOOK! It focuses on the 'apex' of The Mind-Conditioning or Mind Programming process — the remarkable new technique will CONDITION your MIND to bring you everything you want and need... everything you deserve... everything that makes life exciting and enjoyable.

So, the next chapter gives you specific 'tools' for preparing your Mind for the remarkable, life-enhancing experience of The Mind-Conditioning System.

Get ready, because you'll be amazed at how simple it is to dig up all the FREE gold from the goldmine of your own-mind.

Chapter 10
Use... Master-Key To All Riches Wisely

"Do what you can, with what you have, where you are."

— Theodore Roosevelt

On page 91, you'll find the sample Flow Chart, with all the necessary data already plugged in for your convenience. As you may notice, the flow chart is very similar to the ones professional computer programmers might use to solve a problem. At first glance, the COMPUTER-LIKE Flow Chart may seem complicated. But, it really isn't. It's a simple 'tool' or blueprint, if you will, that graphically represents the Mind-Conditioning process. The best and simplest way to apply The Mind-Conditioning System is with flow chart. The flow chart, as you'll notice, includes squares and diamonds, plus flow symbols to lead you through the flow of information that should go through your MIND as you condition it. By following the sequence of operations, you will be following the steps involved in conditioning the Mind to create the state-of-mind needed for automatic fulfillment of your desires.

As a final word of preparation before you begin the life-transforming experience of Mind-Conditioning or Mind-Programming, may I offer one brief suggestion which may provide a clue by which to recognize MASTER-KEY TO ALL RICHES within the flow chart. The clue is this: "EACH SQUARE AND DIAMOND IN THE FLOW CHART CONTAINS A VERY POWERFUL COMMAND TO HELP YOU LEAD YOU TO THE MASTER-KEY TO ALL RICHES."

It's been 25 years since I began researching and practicing The Mind-Conditioning System using the world's first <u>COMPUTER-LIKE</u> Flow Chart for success using Cutting-Edge Technology, and I can honestly say that the flow chart really works if you work it. When you use the flow chart, I suggest you think of your MIND as the computer, and yourself the programmer, and the flow chart as the blueprint you use to communicate or speak with your own MIND. By this procedure, you'll, (as a Mind Programmer) lead your own mind toward total peace of mind and toward the Master-Key to all riches. This is accomplished by following the flow chart's symbols to the appropriate diagrams, then asking yourself the question or performing the recommended action in the diagram.

The main key to the understanding of the Flow Chart lies in the fact that each 'square' and 'diamond' in the flow chart contains a very powerful "COMMAND".

These commands are anchors, or symbols, or triggers words that tell your MIND, "What duties to perform"! All these anchors are very powerful, profound, and carefully 'selected' words or phrases to help you 'condition' your own Mind. All these anchors or triggers are stimulus-response mechanism. They instantly put you in a positive state-of-mind where you experience the sensation of being re-living that command.

For an example, the moment you give yourself the command, GET READY TO CONDITION MIND, your whole mind and body should instantly go into relaxation. The moment you give command CHOOSE 7-MAJOR NEGATIVE EMOTION, the whole picture of each of these enemies should instantly run through your own mind. A time will come when, the minute you see, imagine, visualize, or think about any of the anchors, trigger words or symbols, your MIND will automatically respond by going into that positive 'state-of-mind' and your mind and body simultaneously experience a CHANGE in the physiology!

In that positive 'State-Of-Mind', the whole universe seem to unfold one by one, just as surely as night follows day. In that mental state, you can relate to the perfect system of balance in the universe. You begin to realize just how you can use the greater power in the universe and how to make use of all the infinite, unbounded, creativity inherent in all the spiritual laws of nature. The main purpose of the flow chart is to help you recognize, relate, assimilate and apply the seven spiritual laws of nature.

The <u>COMPUTER-LIKE</u> Flow Chart is basically your blueprint — the plan, the 'tool' for creating this particular state-of-mind known as <u>faith</u>. When you put the flow chart into regular practice, you'll discover that riches of both spirit and the pocket comes for a certainty of purpose and this faith-filled 'state-of-mind' with little or no hard work.

But remember: Before you can experience this particular, positive state-of-mind, you must completely eliminate 7-major negative emotions from your own mind ... for good.

The flow chart is designed and engineered to do just that!

Now that you know the principles of The Mind-Conditioning System and it's FLOW CHART—and all the benefits of their practice and use—you're now ready to proceed! So ... let's get started.

The Step-By-Step Process For Programming The Mind!

(1) "SELECT A TIME"
The Mind-Programming Process should take no more than about 10 minutes daily. So, select a time when you can carve out an undisturbed 10 minutes for yourself. It can be in the day or evening, but should be when you are most alert and at your physical and mental peak. If you are a morning person, do your programming before you go to work. Or, perhaps you prefer late afternoon or just before sleep. The 10 minutes you choose should be compatible with your physical and psychological 'energy' level and your daily rhythms. I've always done my Mind-Conditioning, or Mind-Programming just before going to sleep. If you do the same, it will be the last experience you provide the MIND before sleep. Your Mind will likely take your mental rehearsals and weave them into pleasant dreams. Pay attention to all the 'messages' in your dreams, because they are often 'energies' or blueprints of your future.

(2) Also, if you ever miss a session, don't worry about it; simply make up for it by spending an extra 10 minutes in your next session.

(3) RELAX
Always program your Mind in the most relaxed, unhurried state possible. If it's time for your mind programming session you're rushed or late for an engagement, it's best to postpone the session until you have time to ease-in-and-out of the relaxed state that is so necessary.

Always begin each session by taking 2 or 3 minutes to progressively relax all your muscles. Starting at the top of your head, imagine waves of relaxation flowing through each muscle group—scalp, face, arms, chest, and so on ... all the way down to your feet and toes. Next, take several deep breath, as you allow yourself to experience your Inner-self, your true Self (God-Self). This gets easier with practice, and soon you'll find your own way to deepen your awareness and relaxation. Relaxation is absolutely crucial because it allows you to release more negative energies from your body. This, in turn, enhances your ability to focus mentally. IF YOU HAVE SUCCESSFULLY USED ANOTHER RELAXATION TECHNIQUE IN THE PAST, BY ALL MEANS USE IT FOR YOUR MIND-PROGRAMMING SESSION.

START:

Hold the filled-in <u>COMPUTER-LIKE</u> Flow Chart in both hands. Take a few deep breaths again, relaxing even deeply and feeling the inner peace. Read aloud (so you hear) the trigger words in the first square of the flow chart. This is a command. Repeat those words, "GET READY TO CONDITION MIND". Repeat several times out loud. I want to emphasize that saying, feeling, and sensing these trigger words with your heart is just as powerful as seeing (visualizing) them in your Mind's eye.

Follow the arrow to the next square of the flow chart. This is also a COMMAND. Repeat those trigger words, "CHOOSE 7-MAJOR NEGATIVE EMOTIONS". Repeat several times out loud (so you hear) the trigger words in the second square. Pause for a moment and sense, feel, imagine, or just pretend that you actually SEE these negative EMOTIONS drifting or floating away from the Mind.

With your Mind's eye (this is important), visualize, or sense or feel, or imagine, or pretend that you see Fear, Hate, Jealousy, Superstition, Greed, Revenge and Anger, leaving your Mind and Body for good, one by one, out and away. During the day, as you go about your daily business; every time you notice ANY of the 7-major negative emotions dominating your MIND, simply say the trigger word RELAX several times, and make a deliberate effort to get-rid of that particular enemy out of your mind. You'll feel a sense of CONTROL over your own MIND. You have the power to control your own MIND. That's your God's given right and privilege for having lived this life as a human being. So, use your right.

FOLLOW THE ARROW TO THE NEXT DIAMOND OF THE FLOW CHART:

This is a question. Repeat those trigger words, "ARE EMOTIONS UNDER YOUR CONTROL"? Repeat several times (so you hear) the trigger words in the diamond. Please remember: This question refers only to the 7-major emotions, (as discussed in the book),

The Seven Spiritual Laws of Nature

If you answer "YES" then, proceed to the next diamond. This is a question also. Repeat those trigger words, "ARE THOUGHTS UNDER YOUR CONTROL." This is an extremely important question, because ONLY by controlling your own thoughts, You control your own MIND. This is the only known method of controlling your own MIND. You Control your Mind by Controlling your own thinking. There is no other way at the present.

If you answer "NO", then just follow the "NO" arrow to the square this is again a COMMAND for you, "ELIMINATE SEVEN MAJOR NEGATIVE EMOTIONS". Obey this new command. Immediately repeat this step by asking yourself again, "ARE EMOTIONS UNDER CONTROL"?

FOLLOW THE "YES" ARROW TO THE NEXT DIAMOND OF THE FLOW CHART:

This is again question to yourself, "ARE THOUGHTS UNDER YOUR CONTROL?" If the answer is "YES", then go on to the next square, which is a COMMAND. If the answer is still "NO" then, follow the "NO" arrow back to the diamond, which is a question, "ARE EMOTION UNDER YOUR CONTROL"? As you may have noticed, that all you are trying to do at this early stage of Mind-Conditioning or Mind-Programming is to make sure that you are aware of the fact that you do need to fully and completely eliminate all 7-major negative emotions from your Mind, before proceeding any further. With consistent practice, it will get easier and easier. A time will when the minute you repeat these COMMANDS and QUESTIONS, your trigger words will instantly respond by helping you go into that positive 'State-Of-Mind' and your Mind and Body will simultaneously 'experience' a mental CHANGE in the physiology. It's like having a bit of sun-shine in a room that has been dark and closed for years. When you reach that point in your practice of Mind-Programming, you will then know, that you have arrived to your destination. Now that your own emotions and thoughts are under your own full control the next step is to follow the sequence of the flow chart.

FOLLOW THE "YES" ARROW TO THE NEXT SQUARE OF THE FLOW CHART.

Follow the "YES" arrow to the next square. This is again a COMMAND, "FIX MIND ON MENTAL PICTURE OF YOUR GOALS". This command is the life-blood of the COMPUTER-LIKE Flow Chart.

The whole purpose of using this world's first flow chart is to help you 'define' some goals in life and then reach them by controlling your Mind-Body relationship to 'access' the infinite, unbounded creativity of the mind of nature. Here's what you must do? To help your MIND achieve your goals, you must write them clearly. They could be in any area of your life: personal, professional, spiritual, etc. Do this: Write your own goals for six months and for one year. Write them with a pencil to symbolize the need for changing your mind about your goals and direction as you learn and grow in awareness. This will happen as you continue to practice this COMPUTER-LIKE Flow Chart technique.

Every day, look at your goals. Spend a few moments allowing the words of your goals to move freely through your mind. Always consider the possibility of changing or expanding them. Remember: WISDOM IS FLEXIBLE!

Regular practice of the flow chart technique, plus regular moments of perfect silence, will allow your perfect inner wisdom to come forward into your consciousness. Then it will direct your activity and guide you to your brighter future. PLEASE DO TAKE TIME TO BE STILL AND TO BE GUIDED BY THE PERFECT WISDOM OF YOUR INNER-SELF! Once you have set some goals, it's now time to go to the next step in the sequence of the flow chart.

FOLLOW THE ARROW TO THE NEXT DIAMOND OF THE FLOW CHART!

This is again a question to yourself by your self (called the autosuggestion), "IS MENTAL ATTITUDE NEGATIVE?" If your answer is "YES", you certainly have some more work to do before moving on to the next step in this flow chart. Let me be perfectly frank with you! A very 'definite' "YES" answer to this question simply means doubts about this whole Mind Programming process.

It also indicates, that you have NOT yet fully and completely released from your own MIND one or perhaps more of the 7-major negative emotions. To create a 'state-of-mind' that draws prosperity like a magnet, brings praise and respect from others, saves time and efforts, and enhances personal freedom, you MUST fully and completely eliminate seven major enemies of humankind known as Fear, Hate, Jealousy, Superstition, Greed, Revenge and Anger from your own MIND for good. The presence of even ONE negative emotion in your mind is enough to completely wipe-out ANY chance for programming your mind for success consciousness.

In order to eliminate all seven major negative emotions from your own MIND, YOU NEED TO REPROGRAM YOUR MIND WITH COUNTER-PARTS OR WITH SEVEN MAJOR POSITIVE EMOTIONS. These seven positive counterparts of seven major negative emotions are as follows: DESIRE, FAITH, LOVE, HOPE, CARING, ROMANCE, and ENTHUSIASM! These seven major positive words are, (much the negative emotions words,) the positive anchors, or symbols, or trigger words that tell your MIND what duties to perform. In this case, these seven major positive trigger words will simply replace the negative counter-parts to reprogram the Mind! (These 7-Major POSITIVE EMOTIONS are fully explained in the next chapter).

With this very brief introduction to the positive emotions, let's now get back to the Mind Programming Process. As I have mentioned that if, after several honest attempts, you still answer "YES" to the question in the flow chart, "IS MENTAL ATTITUDE NEGATIVE"?, I suggest you take a few deep breaths and RELAX.

If negative thoughts and emotions creep into your own MIND, just say, "Oh, Well." Try to take full and complete control of your own MIND by controlling your own thinking and feel the peace. I have found that if, after several attempts, my own Mind is still negative, then I don't worry about it. I simply make up for it by spending an extra 10 minutes in my next session. Know this: "It is YOUR determination and efforts to fully control your own Mind that eventually

The Seven Spiritual Laws of Nature

will lead you to the open door of all your wisdom. Is the price worth the effort? You bet!

With my strictest self-control and determination, when I repeat the question in the flow chart, "IS MENTAL ATTITUDE NEGATIVE?", my answer is always a definite "NO". That's because, at this stage of Mind-Programming process, I do feel very calm and peaceful! When answer to this question is "NO" then, I follow the "NO" arrow to the ultimate "SQUARE" (this is my destination). This square is a COMMAND which states: "USE MASTER-KEY TO ALL RICHES WISELY"!

This is indeed, the ULTIMATE power 'secret'. It turns all negative emotions into positive anticipations for peace and prosperity.

I discovered this ultimate power of the MIND using the world's first <u>COMPUTER-LIKE</u> flow chart. This ultimate power eventually WILL reveal to YOU all the secrets and the mysteries of this universe. When you reach to this square on the flow chart, you'll possess the master-key which unlocks the door to that (power) contained in seven spiritual laws of nature.

Moreover, you will control that door so completely, that no undesirable thought, emotion may ever influence your own MIND. The whole purpose of the flow chart is to help your own MIND become a "receiving set" through which ideas, plans and thoughts flash into the MIND.

Most people, by the time they reach the final destination of finding the Master-Key to all riches, report that they are indeed able to eliminate the 7-major negative emotions from their MINDS for good. They're also able to take full and complete possession of their own Minds — simply by controlling each and every thought that enters their Minds, using affirmations and self-suggestions and repeating these trigger words and directing their Minds toward their goals.

If you haven't been able to reach your own final destination of finding your Master-Key to all riches. If you have not yet been able to eliminate the 7-major negative emotions from your own Mind.

If you haven't been able to take full and complete possession of your own Mind. Don't worry. Just continue along the flow chart with strictest of persistence. GO BACK TO THE DIAMOND IN THE FLOW CHART, "IS MENTAL ATTITUDE NEGATIVE?" If the answer is "YES", then follow the "YES" arrow to the square. This is a command, "RUN AWAY FROM ALL NEGATIVE THINKING"! Obey the command and immediately follow the arrow in the flow chart to the diamond, "WAS GET AWAY SUCCESSFUL?" Your answer most likely will be "YES". If so, follow the "YES" arrow to your final destination. If, however, your answer is "NO", then follow the "NO" arrow to the diamond, "ARE MENTAL OBSTACLES IN YOUR WAY"? A "YES" answer here simply means that you still need to work on eliminating the 7-major emotions from your own MIND for good CONTINUE TO FOLLOW THE FLOW CHART UNTIL YOU CAN ANSWER "YES" TO THE QUESTION, "WAS GET AWAY SUCCESSFUL?"

From here on, the flow chart becomes even simpler. Just continue along its course, follow each and every step, the appropriate arrows, answering questions, and obeying all commands.

At first couple of sessions, it may seem a complicated process. But, it really isn't? It's just like anything else you try to learn. In the beginning, it seem almost impossible and then, with practice it's a piece of cake! I know of people who can do it in just minutes. I personally can do it a few seconds. It shouldn't take you more than 10 minutes to do the whole Mind-Programming process.

Just follow each command, answer each question truthfully. You may need to pass through all the questions and commands until you find yourself back at the beginning of the flow chart. If that happens (and it probably will in the beginning), just don't despair if this happens to you. But, please don't give up. Simply restart the whole session, perhaps at a later day, beginning with step 1.

However, it's even more likely that with persistence practice, you won't have to return to "START" on the flow chart. Most people report that some point after the question, "IS MENTAL ATTITUDE NEGATIVE?", they do discover the Master-Key to all riches. When that happens to you, you'll indeed deserve to be proud of yourself. Then your only task is to USE ... MASTER-KEY WISELY!!

If you are among those who have found the Master-Key to all riches, I salute YOU! You are indeed one in a million. It took me 25 years of constant trial-and-error practice to find it. I wish someone had given me the <u>COMPUTER-LIKE</u> Flow Chart. I gladly would have paid hundreds or perhaps thousands of dollars for it — and it would have been worth every penny.

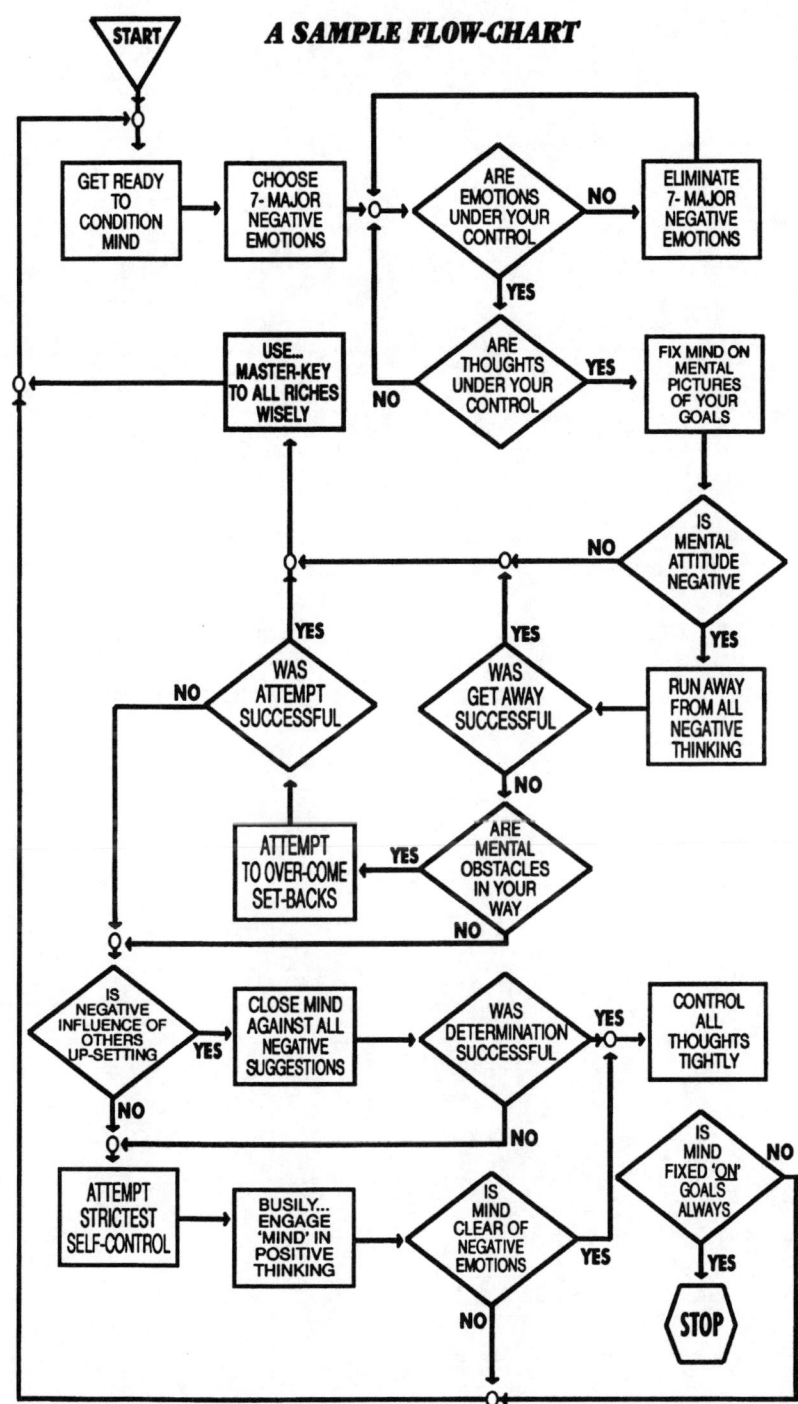

Chapter 11
Nourish Your Mind With The Seven Positive Emotions

"The health of the people is really the foundation upon which all their happiness and all their powers as a state depends."
— Benjamin Disraeli

What is the secret to maintaining a perfect physical body and a high level of health and wellness?

The answer is: By keeping your stress level as low as possible! To do that, you must 'condition' your own MIND to 'release' all stress through a 'creative' channel. This is accomplished by using the COMPUTER-LIKE Flow Chart Concept, which was introduced in the last Chapter. The flow chart works somewhat like a computer program that tells a computer how to solve a problem. The flow chart tells your MIND how to solve the problem of stress and tension in your life. The whole purpose of the flow chart concept is to properly program your mind. Then you'll possess the MASTER-KEY that will allow you to see through your physical body, your own true or spiritual individuality. Then you will recognize, embrace and celebrate yourself, because you will be seeing your true Self the Other Self!

The Other Self is capable of helping the human heart work in its healthy three-phase pattern: two beats for pumping and one beat for resting. When you are tense, stressed or nervous, the heart's two active (pumping) phases keep on working, but the rest phase is either shortened or completely eliminated. If the tension or stress continues over a long period, the heart suffers tremendously and usually 'skips' the third most important beat.

Do you constantly or frequently live with 'stress', tension and nervousness? You are not alone. According to some estimates, 85 percent of all people have stress levels that are much higher than they should be. If you are among the majority, you MUST find a way to 'release' YOUR 'stress' through creative CHANNELS.

The American Academy of Family Physicians estimates that about two-thirds of all visits to family doctors are prompted by stress-related symptoms.

This year, stress alone will add some 75 billion dollars to employer's health care costs. Corporations spend $750.00 annually in stress-related costs for every worker in the United States of America. Experts say stress is a leading contributor to the six most common causes of death in the United States and Canada. Stress is a major cause of heart disease, liver cancer, lung ailments, accidental injuries and even suicide.

How does 'stress' disrupt health? You may ask: Well —— when you don't use some creative channels to 'control' or direct your own negative energies (negative thoughts & emotions), those energies settle into body "pockets", where they can cause congestion, indigestion, muscle spasms and poor body functioning. Emotions may become unbalanced, too, resulting in depression or anxiety. How do I know all this is true? I'll be first to admit I am not a medical doctor. I haven't made any scientific breakthroughs in a laboratory. But I know intuitively these facts are true. You'll surely have all the proof you need as soon as you begin to practice world's first COMPUTER-LIKE Flow Chart for success and health using Cutting-Edge Technology as outlined in this last Chapter.

I am emphatic about the seriousness of 'stress' because, when you allow it to build up in your system, you easily can become a target for a major heart attack or even for a premature death. So releasing 'stress' and other negative energies (both negative thoughts and emotions), could be a 'life-saving' action.

STRESS AND THE MIND-BODY RELATIONSHIP:

The human MIND is engineered and designed to fully control and direct EVERY function and every movement of the human body. It is said that the human heart can very easily function for a hundred or more years. It was engineered to do just that.

Our own MIND, is the only one thing that controls and directs the human heart by allowing the heart to 'work' in a three-phase operation: two beats for pumping the blood through out the body and one beat for resting the heart. When you are stressed, tense, or nervous, the heart's two active (pumping) phases keep on working, but the rest phase (the most important phase) is either shortened or completely eliminated. If the tension, stress or nervousness continues over a long period, the heart suffers tremendously. Under these conditions, the human heart just 'skips' the third, most important, beat and keeps on working (pumping) in just only two active phases. It NEVER has an opportunity for the most important third beat, which allows the heart to rest. How would you feel if you had to be active all the time and could never sleep or rest? That's what happens to your heart if you don't 'release' all that body "pockets" of tension, stress and all other negatives causing congestion, indigestion, muscle spasms and the poor body functioning.

Without doubt the human heart is the most mysterious, the most awe-inspiring product the nature has produced, and at the same time it is the least understood, and most often abused of man or woman's profound gift from our Creator!

For the human heart to give you a life of hundred or more years is but a child's play. Unfortunately, it usually stops short of this time frame because of the negative 'energies' (negative thoughts & emotion) that forces the human heart to remain active and skip one of the three beats. In some cases, these negative energies can completely stop the heart, often prematurely, and cause a fatal heart attack or even a premature death.

UNLESS WE CONTROL PROLONGED PERIODS OF TENSION, STRESS, AND NERVOUSNESS? Unless, we learn to 'release' all stress through some creative channels? It is for sure, that the heart's life expectancy is usually reduced.

And, our own MIND, is the one and only means by which all these negative 'energies' may be released through creative channels.

Now — at this point, you may be wondering what all this has to do with programming the MIND for successful health, peace and total personal freedom. This is where my NEW, world's first <u>COMPUTER-LIKE</u> Flow CHART Concept comes into action. I truly believe, that this Flow Chart Concept will revolutionize the release of stress through a creative channel.

I also believe the Flow Chart Concept, (revealed in the last Chapter), may become an instrument to 'help' the heart function in it's complete three-phase pattern. This concept could help people to develop peace, inner strengths and relaxation. Mostly, it will help them become one with the MIND, Body and EMOTIONS through peace.

The only known method (at the present), for voluntarily releasing all tension, stress and nervousness, through creative channels without the use of any medicine or drug or any other stimulants, is by ELIMINATING THE SEVEN MAJOR NEGATIVE EMOTIONS FROM YOUR OWN MIND!

Furthermore; the only known method (spiritually), for making sure that the human heart, functions in a three-phase operation is through the use of COMPUTER-LIKE Flow Chart for success, health, peace and total personal freedom using Cutting-Edge Technology! In the previous Chapter, we learned how to program the MIND by eliminating the SEVEN MAJOR NEGATIVE EMOTIONS from your own MIND for good.

But, you see; the problem starts, when you completely get-rid of all 7-major emotions from your own MIND, there develops a GAP or seven empty spaces (so to speak) in the MIND. These seven empty spaces, must now be completely 'filled' with the exactly powerful counter-parts. These powerful, energy-boosting counter-parts are called the seven major positive emotions. These seven counter-parts are trigger words, or anchors or symbols that actually RE-PROGRAM the MIND, by filling the "GAP" or the seven empty spaces. AND, THAT'S WHAT THE REPRO-

GRAMMING OF THE MIND IS ALL ABOUT! You simply, force or 'feed' the 7-major positive emotions into the MIND.

Positive and negative emotions cannot occupy the MIND at the same time. One or the other MUST dominate. IT IS YOUR RESPONSIBILITY to make sure that POSITIVE EMOTIONS constitute the dominating influence of your own MIND.

Form the habit of applying and using the 7-major positive emotions! Here the spiritual law of Harmony and Attraction will come to your aid, every time! Eventually, these 7-major positive emotions will dominate your MIND so completely that the negative emotions can not enter it.

Only by following these instructions completely and literally, and continuously, can you 'gain' control over your negative thoughts and emotions. The presence of a single 'negative' in your own MIND is sufficient to destroy ALL chances of any constructive aid from your own MIND. The presence of ALL positive emotions is necessary to REPROGRAM the MIND.

A good many statements in the Chapter on "Use ... THE MASTER-KEY TO ALL RICHES", will be repeated here, for the benefit of your MIND. Remember this: "Your own MIND functions voluntarily, whether you make any effort to influence it or not." This, naturally suggests to you that thoughts of fear, hate, jealousy, superstition, greed, revenge and anger serve as stimuli to your own MIND, unless you master these negative emotions and give it more desirable food upon which it may feed, (such as the 7-major positive emotions). Your MIND will not remain idle! If you fail to plant desires in your MIND, it will feed upon the thoughts and emotions which reach it as the result of your neglect. For the present, it is sufficient if you remember that you are living daily in the midst of all manner of thought impulses which are reaching your Mind, without your knowledge. You are now engaged in trying to help 'shut-off' the flow of negative thoughts and emotions, and to aid in voluntarily influence (REPROGRAM) your mind through seven major positive emotions.

The Seven Major Positive Emotions!

DESIRE:

Desire is the first positive emotion you must 'feed' into your own MIND. All the people who succeed in life usually got off to a bad start and passed through many hardships, struggles and heartbreaks. Through their sheer DESIRE to succeed, they finally "arrived". When desire dwells in your MIND, it propels you forward in life and helps you reach your biggest goals.

FAITH:

The second royal guest you must allow to dwell in the castle of your own MIND is FAITH. You'll not have the DESIRE unless FAITH is tugging in your MIND. NO one is really ready for anything unless he or she believes it can be achieved. If you want your DESIRES to be materialized, feed FAITH into your MIND along with the emotion of DESIRE.

LOVE:

This positive emotion encourages us to love one another and share our blessings with others. The capacity to love and understand others unusually eliminates much of the friction among people. LOVE is the foundation of harmony, friendship, cooperation and all the spiritual laws of nature. You MUST feed LOVE into your own MIND so it will help you assume a NEW more powerful personality.

HOPE:

Hope provides the necessary belief that YOU WILL ACHIEVE YOUR OWN HEART FELT OBJECTIVES. It gives you a deep-rooted enthusiasm to 'channel' all bodily desires into positive, worthwhile outlets. It provides the means of releasing stress, tension, nervousness through creative channels.

CARING:

Caring is more than just an emotion, it's a bond, a rapport or a relationship that connects us with every living being. It instills the thought, "HOW CAN I HELP?" Caring has nothing to do with your own ego, so it never asks, "What's in it for me?" The emotion of CARING is so powerful that whenever it is 'mixed' with LOVE and blended with faith plus hope, it has the power to 'lift' people from lowly places to the ultimate heights of accomplishments.

ROMANCE:

The sixth positive emotion is Romance. There can be no richer person than the one who has been blessed with an understanding spouse. When thing get tough — and you bet they will — or when there seem to be no reason to continue, everything will tell you to give up and quit. But this spouse, through his or her FAITH in you, will give you the support you need to press toward your goals.

ENTHUSIASM:

This emotion is indeed contagious. It helps you gain cooperation from others and, more importantly, it inspires you to draw upon the power of your imagination. Deep-rooted enthusiasm is the lifeblood of all sales organizations. I ought to know, because I was in sales for 15 years. Enthusiasm spurs action and makes going the extra mile a habit.

There they are ... all of the seven major positive emotions, your loyal friends.

We are indeed, ready to plug these seven major friends of mankind into our <u>COMPUTER-LIKE</u> Flow Chart so that we can fill the GAP or the seven empty spaces in our MIND created by the "evil twins"!

I LOOK FORWARD TO RECONNECTING WITH YOU IN OUR NEXT CHAPTER, WHERE WE TAKE A STEP-BY-STEP APPROACH TO REPROGRAMMING THE MIND FOR SUCCESS!

Chapter 12
Capitalize On The ... Power Of Your Other-Self!

"If you would win a man to your cause, first convince him that you are his sincere friend."
— Abraham Lincoln

On page 119, you'll find a typical Flow Chart, with all the necessary data (information) already plugged in for your convenience. As you may notice, that the flow chart is very similar to the one you used to eliminate seven major negative emotions from your own Mind! As you may recall; that when you completely eliminated all 7-major negative emotions from your own Mind for good, there developed a "Gap" or an empty space in your Mind. The purpose of these 7-major positive emotions is to fill that "Gap" or the seven empty 'holes', to reprogram the MIND to Capitalize on the Power of your true Self or the "Other-Self"!

Now you have your blueprint... a plan or tool you can use to to release all stress and tension from your own MIND, so that it can control and direct every function and every movement of the human body. When that happens, the Mind will also control and direct your 'heart' by allowing the 'heart' to work in three phase: two beats for pumping and one beat for resting. As you remember: When you are tense, stressed or nervous, the heart's two active (pumping) phases keep on working, but the 'rest' phase is either shortened or as in many cases, completely eliminated. And, if the tension continues over a long period, the heart suffers tremendously.

It is said, that the human 'heart' can easily function for a hundred or more years. But, in order to survive and live the full intended life's expectancy, the human 'heart' must function in it's three-phase operation: two beats for pumping the blood through the streams, and one for resting. Prolonged periods of tension, stress and nervousness causes the 'heart' to usually skip one of every three beats, and stop the heart prematurely.

With this world's first COMPUTER-LIKE Flow Chart, you now have a tool or your own blueprint or a plan of action to completely release stress and tension so that you can overcome limitations, reach your goal in life and achieve total personal freedom. THAT BLUEPRINT IS THE COMPUTER-LIKE FLOW CHART.

But, the flow chart is just the beginning. It's an outline, a place to start. Next you need a step-by-step process for using this blueprint to reprogram and re-educate your own Mind! WITH THIS PROCESS, YOU WILL CAPITALIZE ON THE POWER OF YOUR TRUE-SELF YOUR OTHER-SELF!

I'm about to share with you the most time-honored and successful Mind-Programming process. It's used by super achievers in almost every major country where progress, personal growth and the entrepreneurial spirit are truly valued. I myself, have used process many many times and believe that it will add more depth and meaning to what you will be doing. Through this Mind-Programming you'll, through daily practice of the following steps, you will 'clear' all negative internal dialogues (self-talk) from your own

Mind. This will reduce tension and stress and make you more 'receptive' to inner health.

At this point, let me stress that you should ALWAYS program your Mind with feelings of joy, happiness and excitement. Your Mind best understands the language of emotions, feelings, joy and excitement, so Capitalize it!

NOW, HERE ARE THE STEPS FOR THE LIFE-ENHANCING, FREEING PROCESS OF REPROGRAMMING YOUR OWN MIND!

A Step-By-Step Process For Reprogramming The Mind!

Select a time.

This process for mind programming should take no more than 10 minutes. So, select a time during the day or evening when you can have undisturbed 10 minutes by yourself. Choose a time when you are most alert and your psychological and physical peak.

If you're a morning person, do your Mind-Programming just before you go to work. Or, perhaps you prefer late afternoon or the time just before sleep. The 10 minute period you choose should be compatible with your physical and psychological energy levels and daily rhythms.

For example, I've always done my own Mind-Programming at night just before going to sleep. If you do the same, it will be the last experience you provide the Mind just before sleep. So your Mind will likely take your mental rehearsals and weave them into pleasant dreams. Pay attention to all the messages you receive in your dreams, because they are often energies or blueprints of the future.

Some people prefer to PROGRAM their MINDS two or even three times a day. Whether you choose once, twice or three times daily, try to stick to the time(s) you select. Avoid changing them unless you must.

Relax:

Always program your mind in the most relaxed, unhurried state possible. If it's time for your Mind Programming session to begin, and you are rushed or late for an engagement, it's best to postpone the session until you have the necessary time to ease-in and ease-out of relaxed state that is so essential to Mind-Programming.

Begin each session by taking two or three minutes to progressively 'relax' all your muscles. Starting at the top of your head, imagine waves of relaxation flowing through each of your muscle groups — scalp, face, neck, shoulders, arms, chest, and so on ... all the way down to your feet and toes. Next, take several deep breaths, 'holding' and then releasing each one. Relax more deeply with each breath, as you allow yourself to experience your inner-Self, your true Self, your "Other-Self"! All of this becomes easier with practice, and soon you'll find your own way to deepen the awareness and relaxation. Know this: Relaxation is absolutely crucial because it allows you to RELEASE more negative energies from your body. This, in turn, enhances your ability to focus mentally. If you have successfully used another relaxation technique in the past, by all means use it for your session of Mind-Programming.

Prepare yourself mentally.

Hold the filled-in flow chart in both hands. Take a few deep breaths again, relaxing even more deeply and feeling the inner-peace! Read aloud (so you can hear) the trigger words in the first command (square) of the flow chart "GET READY TO CONDITION MIND". REPEAT THOSE WORDS SEVERAL TIMES OUT LOUD. I want to emphasize that saying, feeling, and sensing these key trigger words with your own heart is just as powerful as seeing them (visualize) with your mental eyes.

Follow the arrow to "CHOOSE 7-MAJOR POSITIVE EMOTIONS". Pause for a few moments and sense, feel or see with your Mind's eye, these seven emotions (Desire, Faith, Love, Hope, Caring, Romance and Enthusiasm) and feel as though they are are slowly sinking into your own MIND.

Follow the arrow to "IS MIND UNDER THESE EMOTIONS". If the answer is an honest "YES", proceed to the next step by following the "YES" arrow. However; if the answer is "NO", follow the "NO" arrow to COMMAND (square) "FEED ALL 7 MAJOR EMOTIONS" (in the Mind). Obey this COMMAND and repeat the QUESTION (Diamond) "IS MIND UNDER THESE EMOTIONS"? It is imperative that you get a "YES" answer to this question, before proceeding any further.

Follow the "YES" arrow to "IS THINKING UNDER THESE EMOTIONS". If the answer is "YES", go on to the next COMMAND (square) by following the "YES" arrow. However; if the answer is "NO", follow the "NO" arrow to the QUESTION, "IS MIND UNDER THESE (positive) EMOTIONS"? It is imperative that you get a "YES" answer to, "IS THINKING UNDER THESE

EMOTIONS"? If you have to go all the way back, and start the process again, that's fine. Just don't give up!

Follow the "YES" arrow to COMMAND (square), "FIX MIND ON MENTAL PICTURES OF YOUR GOAL". Obey this Command. Put your Mind to work on your goals in life. The object of this is to experience your true Self, and "Other-Self". Remember this: You have a special and unique "talent" to give to others, and this "talent" is so special and so unique that ONLY YOU CAN DO IT BETTER THAN ANYONE ELSE ALIVE IN THIS WHOLE WORLD.

Furthermore; You have a "talent" that is so special and unique that there is no one else alive on this whole planet earth that has the SAME "talent", or that of expression of that "talent". Moreover; there is a unique NEED for your special and unique "talent", and — when this NEED is MATCHED with the creative expression of your own unique "talent", that is when you 'ignite' the spark in the creative MIND of nature, and thus; helps you 'access' to all it's infinite, unbounded creativity.

Remember this always: "Expressing your special and unique "talent" to fulfill your own needs, COULD VERY WELL CREATE AN UN-LIMITED WEALTH AND ABUNDANCE FOR LIFE".

Be sure to Capitalize on the power of your Other-Self! This process begins, once you follow the COMMAND, "FIX MIND ON MENTAL PICTURE OF YOUR GOALS". Only when you have completed this COMMAND, do you go on to the next step.

Follow arrow to the question (Diamond), "IS STATE-OF-MIND NEGATIVE"? If your answer is "YES", you have some work to do before moving on (Be sure to read, "What to do if your State-Of-Mind is negative). However; at this point, your answer is more likely to be "NO", because you are probably calm, relaxed and peaceful if you really have fed the Seven Major Positive Emotions into your Mind. In this case, you can go on to the next step.

Follow the "NO" arrow to, "CAPITALIZE ON THE POWER OF YOUR OTHER-SELF". This, the ultimate goal of your Mind-Programming, is where you recognize, relate, assimilate and apply that (power) of your Other-Self — the part that helps you release all negative energies from your system through a creative channel — so you can achieve total well-being and personal freedom. This is possible ONLY when you experience the universal Oneness within.

WHAT TO DO IF YOUR STATE-OF-MIND IS NEGATIVE?

If your answer is 'YES" to the Question (Diamond), "IS STATE OF MIND IS NEGATIVE"?, take a few deep breaths, relax and try to feel the inner-peace. When you feel able to reconnect with yourself, again ask yourself, if your 'state-of-mind' is negative. If the answer is again "YES", follow the 'YES" arrow and give yourself the COMMAND to, "ATTEMPT STRICTEST WILLPOWER". Then, go to the next question, "WAS ATTEMPT SUCCESSFUL?". If it was, take the "YES" arrow up to, "CAPITALIZE ON THE POWER OF YOUR OTHER SELF"!

If your best efforts are unsuccessful, it means that you are having some doubts about the soundness of the Mind-Programming Process using this world's first <u>COMPUTER-LIKE</u> Flow Chart Concept. Skepticism in connection with all NEW 'ideas' is characteristic of all human beings, but; if the follow the flow chart's instructions as out-lined, your skepticism will soon be replaced by belief, and this in turn, will soon become crystallized into absolute faith. Please do not let the flow chart's simplicity keep you from an ultimate experience of the MIND that could change your life for the better.

However; if your MIND is still negative, it is a good bet that you have NOT fully eliminated one or more of the Seven Major Negative emotions: Fear, Hate, Jealousy, Superstition, Greed, Revenge and Anger. YOU ALSO NEED TO REPROGRAM THE TRIGGER WORD, "FAITH" IN YOUR MIND. Repeat the word "faith" several times! Feel it, sense it with your heart. Let it sink into your Mind slowly until you do feel the sensation or 'tingle' in your body. Now, ask yourself the next question: "IS FAITH IN YOURSELF LACKING?"

Continue along the course of the Flow Chart, following the appropriate arrows to questions and obeying the next commands. You may need to pass through all questions and commands until you find yourself back at the beginning of the flow chart.

Don't despair if this happens. But do not give up, either. Simply restart the session, perhaps at a later time, beginning with the first COMMAND, "GET READY TO CONDITION MIND". However, it is even more likely that you will not have to return to "Start" on the flow chart. At any point, after the question, "IS STATE OF MIND NEGATIVE", you may succeed in discovering your "Other-Self" — and the universal Oneness within you. When that happens, you deserve to be proud of yourself. Now — your only goal and aim is to CAPITALIZE ON THE POWER OF YOUR OTHER SELF!

Most people, by the time they reach the COMMAND to "CAPITALIZE ON THE POWER OF YOUR OTHER-SELF", report that they are able to 'experience' a Universal Oneness. They describe it as a revelation that, at the center of the human Mind, there is a oneness, a presence, or a primal energy (the original universal source) through which they discover that they are ultimately one with all things, as all things are one with them.

When, you too, experience this universal Oneness, you will intuitively agree that it is as if you have become one with the Stars, Nature, all living things and the universe.

Throughout history, a few people have become 'saints' through this ultimate experience of the Minds. But this is not the aim or goal. The aim or goal is to live life more productively by participating more in life, by connecting with others, by establishing human relationships and a universal bond among all human beings.

I earnestly believe that we are now in the process of actively entering into what I call, "The Information Age". And, I further believe that by year 2000, a major cultural transformation in the realm of using these seven spiritual laws of nature will take place. This transformation will be the end result of people like you and I, sharing INFORMATION with each other. I predict that within the new millennium, a universal 'bond' or an international rapport will develop among the people of the world, and here's the reason why? I believe, that human beings were put on this planet to 'connect' with each other. Human beings are the 'greatest' resources we have, and this bond, this rapport will allow us to work TOGETHER to produce results THAT WE COULD NEVER PRODUCE ALONE.

I also believe that this amazing new book on the seven spiritual laws of nature, and the COMPUTER-LIKE Flow Chart Concept may be the very first step to openly and actively invite special people like yourself to the awareness of this cultural transformation by the word of mouth advertisement.

IF YOU ARE ONE OF THE FORTUNATE PEOPLE WHO IS READING THESE LINES THEN CONSIDER YOURSELF LUCKY, BECAUSE YOU MAY BE ONE OF THE CHOSEN ONE'S TO ADVANCE HUMAN PROGRESS BY LEARNING AND TEACHING THE SEVEN SPIRITUAL LAWS OF NATURE TO OTHERS.

If you have not yet 'experienced' this sense of universal Oneness, don't worry. Continue to use the Flow Chart with persistence. Eventually, you will have the experience, and then you will find and know your Other-Self. Once you do find it, you'll know exactly what I am talking about.

On the other hand, if you have experienced this universal Oneness within one-self, I salute you. You are indeed one in a million. It took my 25 years of practice to find my Other-Self. Believe me, it's an unforgettable feeling.

This universal Oneness may last only a few seconds; in that case, it is experienced as "mind expansion". If nothing other than a glimpse of Mind Expansion happens when you practice this flow chart technique, I believe it will be worth all the time and effort you have invested in the mind reprogramming process. And, even if you experience this Mind Expansion only once in your lifetime, it's effect will be a major influence on your own true identity structure and your personality.

When you Capitalize on the enormous power of your Other-Self, you will 'assume' a totally new personality. Your Mind will be quiet and still, as if the Mind and Body are working together in perfect harmony. In fact, that's just what is happening. You have created a relationship between your Mind and Body. Their cooperative efforts help you release stress, tension, nervousness and all negative thoughts and emotions so you can 'experience' total personal freedom ... the freedom that allows you to achieve your highest goals and aims in life.

Well, that's all there is to the process of reprogramming the Mind! As you can see, the flow chart is nothing more nor less than a blue-print, or a 'tool' for having a heart-to-heart talk with your own MIND. You'll look forward to reprogramming your own Mind and you may very well discover things about yourself that you NEVER imagined. Always start each session with joy, happiness and the excitement, this is the language the Mind understand's best!

Let me end the Mind-Programming sessions by sharing this: I earnestly believe that you are entitled to the whole truth behind the seven spiritual laws of nature, and the two **COMPUTER-LIKE** Flow Charts. The many benefits I have received by applying these seven laws of nature, are just too numerous to mention in one volume book, but I'd like to share with you a few of the most dramatic ones. As GOD is my witness, by taking full complete possession of my own Mind, and by eliminating the seven major negative emotions and by feeding the seven major positive emotions, I began to have any thing I wanted, whenever I wanted it. It amazes me how I can meet someone, or read something or go somewhere that often leads me to the fulfillment of the very goal, desire, or aspiration I envision. Sure enough, as GOD is my witness, by digging the FREE gold from the gold-mine of my own-mind and by following the few simple steps as out-lined in the two <u>COMPUTER-LIKE</u> Flow Chart Concept, I began to have anything.

Soon, I was living in a very spacious new ultra-level home that was so luxurious that words cannot describe it!

Since our new home was located near California's famous Mt. Baldy mountain, we had a view that was out of this world! Recently, we spent over $25,000.00 for a custom design landscaping for our backyard. Beautiful and colorful flowers, serenity and peaceful sitting area with breathtaking rock water fall spa touches everyone! The home is now worth more than a quarter of a million dollars. (I turned down an offer for more than that).

And, to top off our new found lifestyle, I bought my wife a mini van so we could enjoy our precious time together. I bought myself a "family car" and a personal car for each of my three sons.

And, to prove to myself that I had finally dug the gold from the gold-mine of my own-mind, (and to make my new neighbors curious about how I was doing so well), I INDULGED IN THE SPORTS CAR OF MY DREAMS!!! And, the gold did not stop there! Soon thereafter, I was offered a very lucrative position with one of Americas largest service type organizations.

Just before the gulf war "Desert Storm", while I was visiting my daughter in the Middle-East, I was offered to teach these seven spiritual laws of nature (with a few variations), to a group of sales professional and I was paid over $10,000.00 in compensation for it. The organization did over $274,000.00 worth of business that month, and 90% of that business was produced by the group of sales professionals I taught these principles. I gave FREE seminars, lectures and courses in the techniques of 'digging' the FREE gold from the gold-mine of your own-mind.

Later, these spiritual laws of nature inspired me to earn a Doctoral Degree in the Science of Metaphysics. Recently, I was mentioned in the Who's Who in Metaphysics, a professional publication. I was the founder of an International Mind-Conditioning Society, an organization devoted exclusively to the teaching of the working principles of the human Mind. My major purpose in life is to establish a scientific laboratory where people from all over the world come to 'connect' with each other, and thus build a lasting bond, report and relationships.

Now — let me be perfectly honest with you!

I don't tell you all this to impress you. Far from it. I tell all this, because it impressed me!!!

Just by learning the few simple spiritual laws of nature, and by applying the few steps to programming my own Mind, I was not ONLY able to pull myself out of that mental pain, misery, depression, the sinking feelings and severe financial crises I was in, but also, I was able to get all the material possessions and things beyond my wildest dreams. More importantly, it gave me health, happiness, peace of mind and the love of my family back.

One of the very first things you'll notice when you start using the seven spiritual laws of nature, is that you'll develop an amazingly strong bond or a close rapport with everyone you meet.

For instance, my family and I visited the showroom of one of the major Honda Auto Dealership in Ontario, California. In that showroom they had this beautiful brand NEW Honda Accord in a limited 25th anniversary addition available only in one special color. It was love at first sight.

About 45 minutes later, we drove away in that beautiful new car, without paying one red cent. Of course; ten days later I paid cash for it.

Now — the idea of buying a brand new car is nothing special, or a big deal but, driving away in that more than $17,000.00 vehicle without paying a red cent is something that is possible only by Capitalizing on the power of your Other-Self, and by paying cash for it, I saved over $10,000.00 in interest charges alone. I used the very same power to buy a very spacious new ultra-level home in San Dimas, near California's famous Mt. Baldy mountain.

Now again, buying a new home is nothing special, people do it everyday, What was so amazing about this transaction? After all, people buy new homes all the time. Well, when I made the offer, the real estate agent said I would not qualify for the huge home loan and refused to accept my down payment deposit. But I got the home anyway! Using the ultimate power of my Other-Self; I also received a Doctoral Degree in the Metaphysical Science. And recently I was mentioned in the "Who's Who in Metaphysics" publication, which cited my 25 years of work in this self-help field.

These accomplishments were incredible because I was just an immigrant from PAKISTAN, who couldn't speak a word of English and had a very hard time getting admitted to some of the most reputable colleges and Universities in the United States Of America.

But, perhaps the biggest 'proof' of the validity of the soundness of the seven spiritual laws of nature, and the application of the <u>COMPUTER-LIKE</u> Flow chart concept, came by writing this one-of-a-kind book to share with you!

In closing, let me say again: "I don't tell you all this to brag, or to impress you, I tell you all this because it impresses me."! If someone like me, with no special and unique "talent" (at least that's what I used to think before), and with all these handicaps can find the Master-Key to all Riches and able to Capitalize on the power of my Other-Self, just imagine, what you can accomplish with all the 'tools', the blueprint I'm giving you! The information in this valuable new book is truly worth millions of dollars, but since it is given to you for a nominal price, chances are you may be inclined to be a little skeptical. (Remind me, if I am wrong).

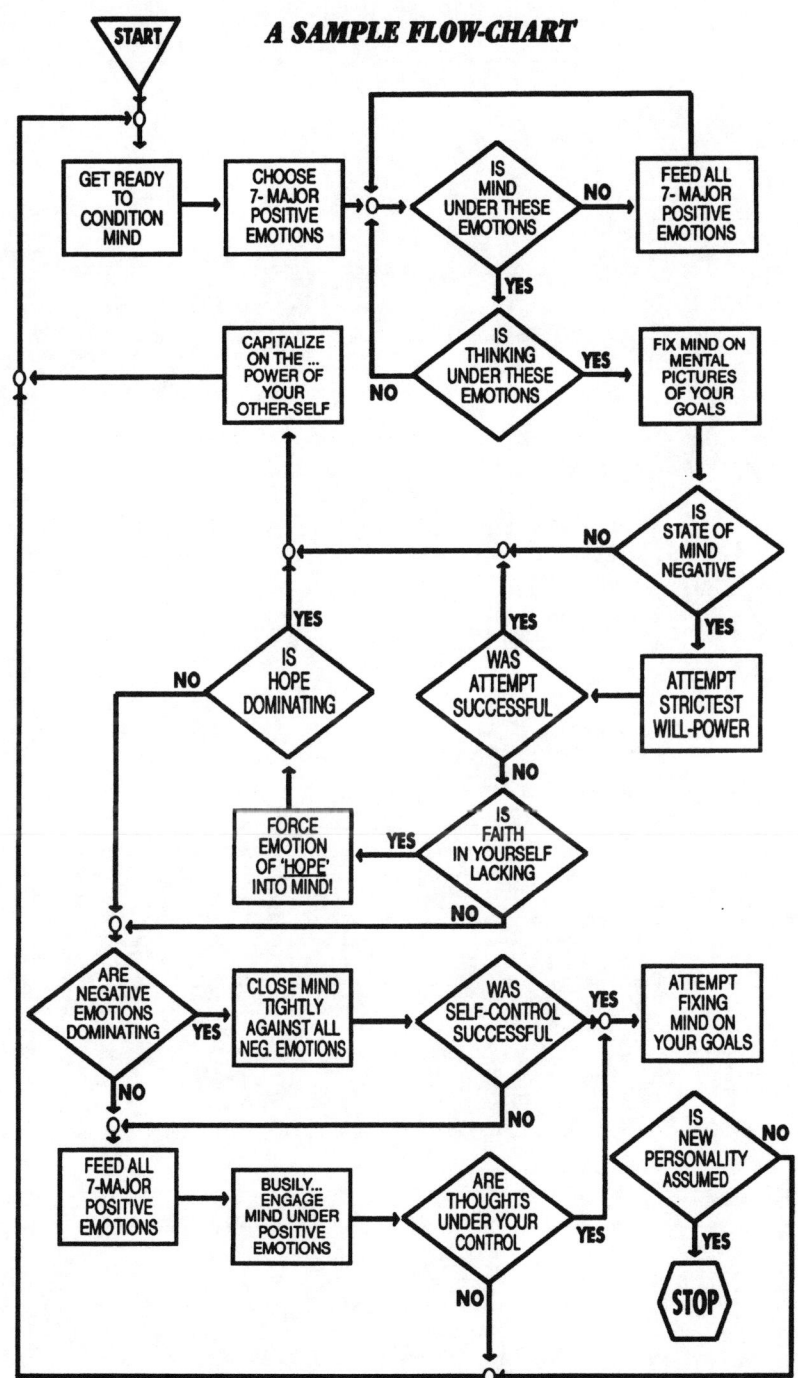

Chapter 13
Increase Your Power By Connecting With Others

"The great end of life is NOT knowledge but action."
— Thomas Huxley

"Don't find fault, find remedy."
— Henry Ford

"Everything that enlarges the sphere of human powers, that shows man he can do what he thought he could not do, is valuable."
— Ben Johnson

Today is the Information Age, when computers, cellular telephones, instant global communications, Satellites and cable TV all reign supreme.

But I see a new kind of Information on the horizon. I earnestly do believe with all my heart, that by the year 2000, a major cultural transformation will be taking place, and it will involve the use of our mental powers. It will be the result of people like you and I sharing absolutely free information with each other. I also predict that the core of all this transformation will be the development of a universal bond or international rapport among the people of the world.

My own 'mission' in life is to form a "CORE" or nucleus of a select group of work-a-day people and Entrepreneurs, who will work together to build a lasting relationship and working together collectively; they will CHANGE THE THINKING HABITS of the masses just like McDonald's CHANGED the eating habits of the people worldwide. I envision about 5000 such people world-wide. Some will be blessed with a more perfect 100% balanced personalities, while others will acquire this perfectly balanced personality by applying the seven spiritual laws of nature and practicing the <u>COMPUTER-LIKE</u> Flow Chart Concept daily.

I would personality like to invite YOU to join me and potentially 5000 others just like you, throughout the world in a 'mission' to make this world strong and wealthy — <u>ONE PERSON AT A TIME!</u>

It's a thrill, you'll NEVER get tired of, I guarantee it!

The seven spiritual laws of nature may be the very first step toward an awareness of this cultural transformation. During my years of study and research to put these seven laws together, I have witnessed many signs of the inevitable, upcoming, massive cultural transformation.

My predictions concerning this massive cultural transformation are based on facts too numerous to describe in one book. However, for the few skeptics who must know, I'll mention the names of some of other people who are also making similar predictions, plus the publications in which I found their evidence of this massive cultural transformation.

For example, one of the most recent prediction came by James Redfield, the author of the mega best seller book The Celestine Prophecy. Mr. Redfield predicts a complete spiritual transformation on earth. I suggest that you buy a copy of that book. You will know exactly what I mean by the upcoming, inevitable massive movement. Napoleon Hill, the author of phenomenal best selling book for the past fifty plus years, "THINK AND GROW RICH", established a foundation for the promotion of his 13 success principles.

W. Clement Stone, the author of, "SUCCESS THROUGH A POSITIVE MENTAL ATTITUDE", formed a foundation in Chicago, with a goal of making this world a better place in which to live. And, Dr. Deepak Chopra, the author of national best seller book, "The Seven Spiritual Laws Of Success", has established a Global Network for spiritual Success. He invites people to join him and potentially millions of others world wide, in his Global Network For Spiritual Success, which is based on the daily practice of these powerful guiding principles. Participation in the Network is open to anyone. He plans to gather a critical mass of successful people who could transform life on earth. (A critical mass is the minimum number of items, in this case people, needed to start a chain reaction, in this case cultural transformation).

It is interesting to note, that I wrote the manuscript of the seven spiritual laws of nature back in 1978. But, I was too LAZY to have it published. I tried to have it published through the regular publishing houses, but letters of rejections after rejections literally poured in from every conceivable publishing house in America. Being human, it hurt my ego. And, that was the end of my writing career.

When I studied the Dr. Deepak Chopra's magnificent book on the seven spiritual laws of success, I began to have the guts again to continue my own 'mission' to be a part of this inevitable massive cultural transformation movement.

One of the most amazing thing these seven spiritual laws of nature has taught me is that, "Nothing in my own life happens just as an accident."

Back in 1978, very few New York publishing houses truly accepted the full significant and the impact the computer cutting-edge technology was about to have in our daily lives.

Perhaps; that's why, most major New York publishers were unwilling to take the risk of publishing my new book. Thank goodness; that such ultra short run printers as Morris Publishing exist, to help authors that may not be published initially by a publishing house, especially that of a newcomer, a publishing house may hesitate to publish it. Self-publishing has become one of the fastest growing segments of the publishing industry.

Being a student of these seven spiritual laws of nature, I always 'watch' for these so-called coincidences in our daily lives.

I know for a fact, that my so-called daily coincidences, or just 'chance' happenings in my daily life are NOT mere coincidences or chance happenings but, they are usually brought to my attention to complete a picture, or perhaps give me a 'clue' or a missing link of some yet unaccomplished goal or purpose or aim in life.

That's why, when during that fateful December 1997, I received my first copy of the Writer's Digest magazine, and I had the urge to write to Morris Publishing and ask for the FREE step-by-step Self-Publishing Guide. Believe me, when I tell you that I learned more from this 112-page guide than all the self-publishing books I read or courses I took in the publishing industry. I knew, right then and there, that this was the co-incidence I was looking for.

The Writer's Digest magazine also inspired me to go back on the drawing board, and rework my manuscript to be worthy for the entry into NATIONAL Self-Published Book-Award contest.

When these seven spiritual laws of nature are incorporated into our consciousness, we will be empowered to create unlimited wealth with effortless ease. And we will experience success in every endeavor because these are the very same laws nature uses to create everything in material existence — everything we can see, hear, smell, taste, or touch.

As knowledge of seven spiritual laws of nature spreads, our culture will be altered in a dramatic way. More of us will discover something new about human life: the real purpose of our existence here on planet Earth. And, as we collectively 'focus' our own attention on the seven spiritual laws of nature each and every day, it won't be long before we reach a critical mass of people who will start the massive cultural transformation on our planet Earth. I predict that, by year 2000, we will see a dramatic growth in the number of people who are conscious of these seven spiritual laws of nature. How else can I explain my deep-rooted belief to share this self-knowledge with others, and all the coincidences that have finally guided me to the Self-Publishing field.

I believe that during this new millennium, more and more people will become conscious and aware of these coincidences or chance-happenings in their own lives. More and more people will be watching for these coincidences on a daily basis. And, by religiously following these coincidences, people will be guided toward their own purpose or perhaps 'mission' in life. These people will learn to follow each and every coincidence they encounter, and over-ride their own reasoning, now matter how sound or logical it appear to be at the moment. This growth will continue until we reach the critical mass necessary to 'set' the new cultural transformation in motion.

Then, the entire culture will begin to take these seven spiritual laws of nature seriously. More people will ask, "What mysterious process underlies human life?" Of course; the true answer underlies in these seven spiritual laws of nature, and the world's first <u>COMPUTER-LIKE</u> Flow Chart Concept will become a vehicle to take you to the final destination.

Now — here's the clue to when this world-wide cultural transformation will take place: "When enough people ask this question AT THE VERY SAME TIME, (day or night), that is when our cultural transformation will surely begin to <u>shift</u>."

I thank my lucky star that I live in America, where people are not put in the "Slammer" because they are helping to start a new cultural transformation. I also thank my lucky stars because I now live in California, especially in Los Angeles, because as I studied the history of Los Angeles City during my 25 years of research and studies, I discovered, with profound interest that, practically every major spiritual movement got their start in this unique city of Los Angeles, where people from all back-ground, race, color and religions reside with perfect harmony, respecting each others beliefs. I'm also grateful that I have been compelled to ask the question, "What mysterious process underlies my own life?" I found my answer in the seven spiritual laws of nature. They have led me into glorious paths of adventure, rekindled an appreciation of true greatness, encouraged creative endeavor, and emboldened the expression of honest thought. I invite you to join me, as a teacher or a student and become an integral part of the critical mass needed to 'shift' our cultural transformation for the betterment of all humankind.

Recently, I got my proof (actually my shock), of the inevitable, up-coming, massive cultural trans-formation movement, and especially the proof of Los Angeles City being the place to start any spiritual undertaking.

There is a new Radio station in the Los Angeles City called the "Personal Achievement Radio". It is KYPA RADIO, and can be found on the 1200 AM dial on the Radio. This radio station is ALL POSITIVE talks all the time. It runs programs on success skills, business skills and healthy life-styles 24 hours a day, seven days a week. You can personally hear some of the highly motivational speakers giving you the smart tips on how to be 'positive' and achieve success through a positive mental attitude. There is NEVER any negative talk of any kind on this Personal Achievement Radio in Los Angeles City. In fact, their logo or advertising statement is, "GIVE US 21 MINUTES A DAY, AND WE WILL CHANGE YOUR LIFE — GUARANTEED"!

This Radio gives away several hundreds dollars worth audio tapes on personal motivation, from some of the highly acclaimed motivational speakers in the field, absolutely FREE. All you have to do to receive these valuable free tapes is to remember the daily quotes from world's famous successful people, when called on the phone.

How do I know all this to be true, well — for one thing, I am also considering the possibilities of creating my own program on KYPA Radio for the promotion of these seven spiritual laws of nature. We are almost through with this one-of-a-kind, amazing new book, I earnestly believe that this valuable book will not be complete without sharing with you my latest research and findings. So permit me to give you a few incidents that might help you to 'accept' all that is mentioned in this book.

If you followed all the instructions given in the last 12 Chapters carefully and faithfully then, you of course know that you have TWO DISTINCT PERSONALITIES within you! One is called the "Personal-Self", and the second is called the "God-Self", and the whole function of these seven spiritual laws of nature, and the world's first COMPUTER-LIKE Flow Chart Concept is to allow your two personalities to work together in harmony as partners.

My own proof of the soundness of the validity of my own two personalities came again just recently. I was listening to the new Radio Station KYPA in Los Angeles, California. This radio station had a highly motivational speaker who was telling a real life incident. He told about a medical doctor who worked in the hospital's emergency turmoil department or ward. This was the place where people were brought in after a fatal auto accident, or a major heart attack. All people brought in this particular emergency ward were usually in severe critical conditions, even to the point of death.

You have probably seen this on a television in some of those hospital emergency room shows, where a person is brought in the operating room. He or she is then, hooked to some EKG or EEG machines and with the electrical electrodes, given a quick electric shock with the hope of retrieving the heart beat and pour life into the body again.

The Seven Spiritual Laws of Nature

On a television show you see a person holding two disks, one in each hand, with wiring hooked up to an oscilliscope where they could see the heart pulse. Suddenly, the attending physician or doctor hits the the two disk—boom—and repeats aloud, one, two and three—boom—again on the unconscious person's chest one on each side, and you see the body literally 'jerk' up with each electrical shock, as the disk hit the chest. If you have ever seen a TV show, you know exactly what I'm talking about.

This is what this medical doctor did for a living. Each and every day working in the emergency room, trying to put life back in the human body. Many times the people would suddenly die and he could verify their death by seeing a very straight line on the oscilloscope with a beep on the screen indicating that the person was indeed dead. And, then he would witness, that a few minutes later, some of the human bodies would come back to life, with no apparent explanation. He would notice, that there would be a loud 'beep' on the screen, with a definite pulse in the human body, and the peaks on the EKG or EEG machine showing the heart beating at full speed again.

He saw this phenomenon over and over again in the emergency operating room. At first, he thought that it was just a coincidence, and all those who got their heart beat back and became alive again, were just happen to be lucky people to get their lives back.

But, it happened too many times to ignore this phenomenon!

So, the doctor started his own private research to find some answer to this so called miracle.

This doctor would visit, during his holidays or week-ends, all those who had died once for all logical and medical reasons but, came back to life again.

This doctor would visit all those people and asked each and every one the same question, "tell me, what did happen during the time you were a dead person?"

No-one had ever asked this question before, but this doctor wanted to know the answer. He visited as many people he could find to ask this question for his own private research. During the course of his own research to find the answers, he visited over 50 people who had apparently died in his emergency operating room in the hospital he worked in those days and witnessed these people coming back to life again.

He asked the very same question, tell me exactly, "What happened when you died?" And, "How did you come back to life again?" He asked this question to each of the 50 or more people he visited for his own private research.

To his amazement, nearly, everyone he asked the same question, gave him the identically the same answer: They all said, that as you (doctor) were trying to give us the electrical shock with the hope to put back the life into our bodies, by starting the heart to beat again, suddenly we found ourselves coming out of our own physical bodies. It appeared, as though we were not a physical beings, instead we were a spiritual beings, we saw ourselves, as coming right out of our own physical bodies, and suddenly we were in the air above you in the operating room, over our beds where you were performing your duties.

We were saying, "hey" doctor — we are here, just above you, everything is "OK", not to worry. Apparently, you could not hear us, we could see that you and your staff were busily engaged in trying to start the beat to work again. We could see no pulse on your EKG or EEG machine the screen showed just a straight line with a loud beep.

And, then suddenly, we saw our whole life span pass right in front of our own eyes, just like an instant replay of a movie on a video tape. We saw the whole life pass with millionth of a second speed. We saw everything we did from the very first day we were born in a house or a hospital to the day we were brought to your operating room. We could witness all the good things we did in life, as well as each and every bad deed we did one-by-one.

They said, it was amazing how we dominated our Mind and Body with negative thoughts and emotions. They could see just how they allowed among other negative things, the emotions of Fear, Hate, Jealousy Superstition, Greed, Revenge and Anger dominate their own Minds.

They all agreed on one thing: They wished they had among other things, allowed, LOVE, and the other positive emotions enter their Mind and Body more often — and they had done something to serve humanity in some small ways for that was the essence of human life, "to serve mankind".

Then, after a while suddenly (they all agreed) they were pulled upward toward what seemed to be heavens above toward the layers of the dark blue skies with the speed of lightening — and when they all arrived at the top, they all saw a brilliant light — it was of such a magnificent power shining over them that they could not face the brilliance of the light.

They were asked several questions — the two most remembered question were: (l) "Who Is Your Creator"? (2) "What did you learn from your life?" They said, immediately after their questions and answers sessions, they were told that it was not their time to come-back yet. Right after that message, we sent back into our life and into our physical bodies, where you had left us, pronouncing us being dead. The "GAP", between the time we were dead and became alive, is the period spent facing our CREATOR.

I must admit, that listened to this speaker on the Personal Achievement Radio, in Los Angeles, I observed that while listening to this speaker on the radio, I was lifted to a high level of mental stimulation. I could visualize the possibility of facing my CREATOR and these few questions. This was remarkable because neither the doctor nor the speaker was any spiritual leader or metaphysical professional. He concluded his speech with the remarks that what he had learned from this doctor's research was that (1) We are a physical as well as spiritual beings. (2) We are given at least two questions to answer with a final examination and take home work.

This speaker, also gave me the proof I was looking for, about our TWO DISTINCT PERSONALITIES.

If you have had such an 'after-death' experience, or if you know of someone who underwent this 'after-death' knowledge in his or her own life, please do let me know. I would love to hear from you about any 'after-death' experience, no matter how small or insignificant may appear to you, so we could share that knowledge with others in the future through our Mind-Conditioning Society!

The second incident I want to share with you deals with the human Mind and Body relationship:

This story really and truly touched my own life. Everything I heard made sense to me, moreover: I could relate every fact to my own life. This is a story about another medical doctor, who was at the time the Dean Of Harvard Medical School. His name is Dr. Richard C. Cabbot. This story is about a talk Dr.

Cabbot had given to the Massachusetts Medical Society (MMS). It seemed that Dr. Cabbot had been involved in an autopsy on a man who had been killed instantly in an automobile accident.

The man on whom Dr. Cabbot did the autopsy was a man, as they say so often, never had a sick day in his entire life. He never took a day off from work for any illness or sickness.

Dr. Cabbot and his team of experts doing the autopsy on that man discovered that the man had massive scar tissues within his body that showed that his body had experienced, and did 'heal' itself from all sorts of health problems including such conditions as cancer and various other illness. And, at that very moment of his autopsy, the doctor said that this man had at least four other fatal and unusual diseases.

Dr. Cabbot, in his autopsy report to the Massachusetts Medical Society said, that this man's body system had set-up some kind of 'defense' that render four unusual fatal diseases harmless. And, all of that the man had never known it.

As result of this autopsy, Dr. Cabbot went on to consider the possibility and ultimately to report his conviction to the (MMS) society that every human body has super wisdom which is always biased in favor of human life rather than death. And, that most of the health problems, difficulties, diseases or ailments we have throughout our life never know about, never experience, because of this tremendous 'healing' process within us that is always going on inside of our own body.

Dr. Cabbot had been shocked and gone into a certain amount of research as a result of this autopsy, and discovered some insights which were certainly shocking to his colleagues and confidantes. This is a very important insight, certainly coming from who is NOT oriented toward spirituality, or religion or the metaphysics but, who certainly is medically pragmatic in the field of surgery and medicine. Dr. Cabbot summed up his report by saying that, "Body is in favor of life, favored in life, biased in favor of life, rather than death.

Dr. Cabbot went on to say that this 'powerful' force within human body is ten times as powerful as any medicines or imitations. He was asked, "What is this powerful force within the body?" Somewhat hesitantly and unblushing he said, "IT WAS GOD"! He said that the 'healing' power on which all of us depend to be alive IS A DIVINE POWER OR WISDOM WITHIN US.

Dr. Cabbot went on to say that he earnestly recommends the medical profession to let the patience know of this great power.

Dr. Cabbot said that it certainly does the medical no good to avoid the word — GOD — then why not teach the people the truth. He said, addressing to his colleagues that all of us should let the patience know of this great force that is working within us — working on both the patience and the doctor side.

After hearing Dr. Cabbot's autopsy report, I could truly relate to everything he said about the powerful force within all of us, that is in favor of life, biased in favor of life rather than death. You see, I too, never had the sick day in my life. The fact is, that for the last fifty plus years, I have never seen the inside of a hospital room. Don't get me wrong, I was in hospital to see my wife, when she had our children, and I visited hospital whenever my friends and colleagues had an operation. But, speaking for myself; I have never been inside a hospital room for any reason. It's hard to believe that for the past fifty some years, my body was never attacked by any disease, or suffer a minor heart attack here and there but, I can honestly say that this powerful 'healing' force within me has always been greater than any disease or ailments. I can not assume that for the last fifty plus years I did not have any health problems, difficulties, diseases or ailments. But I can say that I have never experienced them.

Several years ago, I had this severe pain in my stomach. I just could not get rid of this pain. Being a student, I began to summon the seven spiritual laws of nature for help. Lo and Behold a weeks later, three large kidney 'stones' came out of body as I went to bath room. I have several times sensed a minor heart attack coming, again, I summon the spiritual laws of nature, and there goes the pain in my chest.

Most people still think that I am at least twenty years younger than my real age. In fact, I have a hard time, getting the senior citizen discounts in restaurants and movies. They ask for my identification. (I love it). My friends think I work out daily and go to gym every day for physical exercise. The only exercise I ever do is the mental rehearsals of positive affirmations daily.

Dr. Cabbot certainly reaffirms everything I knew already about the human Mind Body relationship. But, most importantly; Dr Cabbot gave me the proof I was looking for to document in my manuscript. If you have an exceptional health incident and you want to share with The Mind-Conditioning Society, please do let me know!

It was just a co-incidence, that these two stories were available for my research, right at the time of need while writing this chapter of the book. I'm telling you. Things happen so fast, when you are under the spell of these seven spiritual laws of nature.

In parting, I would remind you that previously you may have had a logical excuse for not having force life to come through with whatever you asked, but that alibi is now obsolete, because you are in possession of both, the MASTER-KEY TO ALL RICHES, and the power to "CAPITALIZE ON THE POWER OF YOUR OTHER-SELF". This masterkey is intangible, but it is powerful! There is a reward of stupendous proportions if you put the key to use. It will allow you to conquer self and force life pay whatever you ask. The reward is worthy of your effort. Will you make the start and be convinced?

"It's a funny thing about life; if you refuse to accept anything but the best, you very often get it".

— W. Somerset Maugham

INTERNATIONAL MIND-CONDITIONING SOCIETY
Post Office Box 4157
San Dimas, California 91773

WANTED: TEACHERS AND STUDENTS

Dear Friend:

Now that I've completed the Seven Spiritual Laws Of Nature, I seek a limited number of qualified Professionals with Entrepreneurial abilities who are interested in a joint business venture to promote this philosophy on a world wide basis.

This is a once-in-a-life time opportunity for everyone engaged in the self-help or personal-development field. It offers a chance to serve others by sharing this unique philosophy of individual achievement. Financial rewards are limited only by our imagination, as long as our combined effort is enthusiastic and whole-hearted and we are willing to find ways to share this one-of-a-kind program with others.

Successful candidates must have the following qualifications:
- Willing to learn these seven spiritual laws of nature as outlined in this book.
- Willing to teach this new philosophy to others, either locally or nationwide.
- Experienced in setting up and operating a center of higher educational learning.
- Experienced in giving lectures, conducting seminars or running a correspondence school.
- Teacher with a positive mental attitude toward life in general and toward fellow human beings in particular.

These select candidates will also act as a board of directors, and they will work together to guide the day-to-day operations of this California-based organization. Our long-range goal is to establish a scientific laboratory where people can come from all over the world to attend sessions in "Sitting For Creative Ideas."

EVERYONE INVITED

In The Seven Spiritual Laws Of Nature, I describe the very same universal laws, and The <u>COMPUTER-LIKE</u> Flow Chart Concept that have helped me and countless others to achieve spiritual satisfaction and material success.

I'm writing to invite you to join me and potentially thousands of other world-wide, in the International Mind-Conditioning Society, which will be based on the daily practice of these seven spiritual laws of nature and conditioning the Mind using the <u>COMPUTER-LIKE</u> Flow Chart Concept. The International Mind-Conditioning Society is an organization devoted exclusively to the teaching of the working principles of the human Mind. The main object of this worldwide organization is to draw upon the knowledge of some of the gifted, and genius people and to utilize their special and unique talents to serve humanity.

Participation in the Society is free and is open to anyone who chooses to join me and others in an effort to reach a critical mass to 'set' the new cultural transformation in motion by year 2000. To join the International Mind-Conditioning Society all you need to do is send in your name, address and, if you like, phone number to: INTERNATIONAL MIND-CONDITIONING SOCIETY, Post Office Box 4157, San Dimas, California 91773 U.S.A.

Chapter 14
Summary And Conclusion

Let me sum up everything we have covered so far, by telling you a little story!

A beautiful radiant butterfly, floats gently through the trees, in a deep carpeted forest. It lights upon a golden flower, it's wings softly beating. It lays it's eggs upon a leaf. The eggs hatch into a tiny and ugly caterpillar.

The caterpillar does not know that it has the talent of becoming a gorgeous butterfly. It springs a strong, sturdy cocoon. True! The cocoon protects it but; it also imprisons it. The caterpillar will never be a butterfly, furthermore; it will never realize it's full potential, until it breaks the bonds of it's prison. A prison that made for itself. Eventually, the caterpillar free itself. Becomes the gorgeous butterfly and flies free.

You, as the participant in The Mind-Programming system using the world's first <u>COMPUTER-LIKE</u> flow chart, using the cutting-edge technology for success, have taken a giant step toward freeing yourself, toward living up to your own full potential.

Let me give you a brief preview of what you can expect to gain when you start applying The Seven Spiritual Laws of Nature. The very first spiritual law of nature, compares the MIND with the 'solar system' of this universe. Shows you how to control the MIND by simply 'fixing' your own thoughts toward the mental pictures and images of your own aim or goal in life.

The second spiritual law of nature reveals the means by which your own MIND becomes a 'connecting' link between your MIND and that (power) of the universe.

The third spiritual law of nature deals with a 'miracle' which contains a PASSWORD capable of making you free and helping you appropriate all the great riches of life such as peace-of-mind, health and financial prosperity.

Fourth spiritual law of nature shows you a unique new success proven formula in action, which may make it possible for you to condition or program the MIND for success, using a higher power. Fifth spiritual law of nature, opens the door to the temple of wisdom, known as the sixth sense.

The sixth spiritual law of nature asks the two most important questions that will surely help you find your own purpose or perhaps your own mission in life and, guide you step-by-step and shows you how to accomplish it.

Seventh spiritual law of nature is the 'apex' of this philosophy. It can be assimilated, understood and applied only by first mastering the other six laws of nature.

Next, you are introduced to the world's first <u>COMPUTER-LIKE</u> flow chart for programming the MIND for success, using a new cutting-edge technology for success. By doing these two mental exercises, you'll learn to KNOW yourself to the degree where certain unconscious elements of the super-conscious MIND (Mind of nature) become ONE with you. You'll, thus 'experience' as being one with stars, all things living and the nature.

This is a remarkable achievement of just one volume book, yet all these benefits are yours when you make a commitment to take the steps to put these spiritual laws of nature into effect. When you read this volume book, read as IF I, were your personal friend and writing to you and YOU alone.

If you follow my suggestion in spirit as well as in action, you'll be rewarded with a form of riches sufficient to give you a well balanced life, freedom form all fears and peace-of-mind which shall endure, and ease the trials and stress of living, while preparing you to the accumulation of all material riches in abundance.

But, mostly; it will 'condition' your MIND to get the most benefits from the things that follow. Alright! What follows?

As you begin to understand all seven spiritual laws of nature, you will begin to 'focus' on your true purpose in life, which will lead you to the two big questions, "Who am I?" and "What can I do in this world?" Through the use of the COMPUTER-LIKE flow chart, you'll learn the genius of nature's intelligence. These are the thoughts of GOD — the rest are just details.

You'll learn that you have a purpose in life — a unique gift — or a special talent to give to others. And, you can express your unique and special talent and fulfill the needs of your fellow human beings. You begin to create whatever you want, whenever you want it.

Soon you'll discover, that your life has become an expression of GOD'S thoughts. This will be the essence of your true Self.

The whole purpose of The Seven Spiritual Laws Of Nature — and mental exercises is to help you utilize your own full potential — free you from the bondage of the self-imposed 'Cocoon', which has imprisoned you — and allow you to become the beautiful, radiant butterfly, GOD intended for you to be.

If you are like every human being I know, you are searching for solutions to problems and you can use some help.

Like all of us, you tried many avenues, sought advice from many people and yet most of the problems remain. Well - WE BELIEVE IN YOU!

We believe that, the solution to ANY problem, in any area of your life 'exists' within YOU! As you gain experience with the MIND-PROGRAMMING — you'll learn that, THIS IS SO. In the mean time, I know that no one likes to face problems and troubles alone. Friends, and relatives can sometimes offer short term help just by being there and by listening but; you must remember that they have their own worries, there own unresolved problems and troubles to deal with.

As a member of The International Mind-Conditioning Society, you can be certain, that every other member, our director and staff members understand you and have compassion and offer support while you are in the process finding your answers to the riddle of life.

As the popular 'slang' expression goes, "WE KNOW WHERE IT'S AT?" Why — Because we all have been there. We all have bruises, and scars from life, JUST AS YOU HAVE. You are NOT alone. Every member is dedicated to helping you — help yourself! When you have been a member for some time, you too will feel and profit by the same dedication.

The Seven Spiritual Laws of Nature

MEN AND WOMEN OF ALL AGES ARE WELCOME TO MEMBERSHIP — especially those people in the golden years, to help and support the young ones.

In closing, let me say this: That you have the greatest 'gift' that anyone on earth could have the very same 'gift' that we all have — THE GIFT OF LIFE ITSELF!
Life is a precious gift from our creator, and what we make of life is our gift back to our creator.
The amazing thing is, that so many of us erect of our own prison and LOCK ourselves in.
We construct the highest walls around ourselves. Maximum security it is called. No one can penetrate those walls. No one can get to us. For a while, we are content in our self-made prison. We feel secure but; after a while, we feel bored. We get tired getting up in the morning, going to bed at night, going through the same routine—year after year—really going no where.

Then, we begin to rebel. We want out—the walls we erected to keep others out, keeps us, from getting out. We feel stifled, we feel enraged. We forget that the prison is of our own creation. No one put up the walls, which forbade us from going out — no one — but, ourselves. We rage and fume! Forgetting where we hid the KEY.
So—if we do not find the key—which is within ourselves all along, we remain prisoner of our own self-imposed limitations. Please believe me when I tell you that The 'key' you'll find within these seven spiritual laws of nature—that the COMPUTER-LIKE flow chart will literally CHANGE your life. This self-knowledge can and will turn your own MIND around, from failure to success—from rejections to friendship—from

timidity to self-confidence—from self-conscious to self-esteem.

DO YOU HAVE PROBLEMS THAT DEFY SOLUTION? I mean business problems, money problems, people problems, marriage problems, then you'll want to read this amazing book time after time, whenever you are faced with a problem or a difficult decision.

If you are trying to decide how to deal with SORROWS, STRUGGLES or any CHANGE in your life, then these seven spiritual laws will be of enormous help to you in strengthening your decisions.

If you want to reduce stress, tension, frustrations, nervousness that cause most major illness, or if you want to control anger, excitement or heart stroke, or if you want to control negative thoughts and emotions then, this book is a must reading for you. If you want to have a calm, relaxed attitude, peace-of-mind and better health then you can't afford to take this message lightly.

This amazing new book represents over twenty five years of experience and you'll have all this wealth of self-knowledge behind you — and by the time you finish doing both mental exercises, everything will fall into place.

It is at this point that you begin to truly understand your true Self that God-Self. Moreover; it is at this point you can truly recognize relate, assimilate and apply the holy scripture quotation, "AS A MAN THINKETH OR BELIEVETH IN HIS HEART, SO IS HE."

Now — you WILL succeed, because you know you WILL.

As you apply The seven spiritual laws of nature, please apply them faithfully and exactly as directed.

You'll soon be pleasantly surprised by what appears to be, "A NEW YOU" — emerging from your own self-made Cocoon!

But, you know something? It's NOT a New You at all. It's simply the New YOU — you never allowed to be released before. It's the you, that thought that you could not relax — could not succeed — could not meet people — could not solve any problems — could not be happy — could not be wealthy.

One of the main reasons that you thought, you could not, because most of your life, people have been telling you, YOU CAN'T DO IT. YOU CAN'T HAVE IT. YOU CAN'T BE ANYTHING.

So — you in turn have found it easy to slip into the habit of saying to yourself, "I CAN'T DO IT". "I CAN'T HAVE IT" or "I CAN'T BE THAT", instead of saying to yourself, "I CAN, I CAN".

But, can you really do it? You always think that you know the odds against succeeding — but, did you know the odds in favor of succeeding.

One last word: You are not a failure, simply because you are not wealthy at present, or do not own a fancy car or a big home. There are many kinds of success in life besides; material success.

But; YOU ARE A FAILURE, IF YOU NOW DO NOT BEGIN TO DEVELOP THE VAST POTENTIALS WITH-IN YOU!

You MUST try to do your level best to reach whatever reasonable goals you have in your own MIND.

So long for now my good friend!

Remember we believe in you. You have come a long way. You should be congratulated!

I wish, I might tell you that this one book will solve all your problems or troubles. Frankly, this self-knowledge is just the beginning of your life-long search to find some answers to the real purpose of having lived this life as a human being.

As Dr. Deepak Chopra says most eloquently in his mega best selling book, The seven spiritual laws of success, and I quote: "Everyone has a purpose in life... a unique gift or special talent to give to others."

"And when we blend this unique talent with service to others, we experience the ecstasy and exultation of our own spirit, which is the ultimate goal of all goals."

You, my friend, do have very real purpose in life, for which only you were chosen to give to the world. This purpose mainly deals with service to humanity. I wish I might feel privileged to tell you how you'll find it. But, that would deprive you of much of the benefit you'll receive when you make the discovery in your own way. I have given you many clues in this book.

I'm not going to make you guess, really. But, telling you outright might ruin the surprise, and you wouldn't be given the boost you need to get started on your way. I'm going to give you a little shove in the right direction.

On page 148, I'm giving you a list of MUST READING books that will tell you about your own purpose or perhaps 'mission' in life in a variety of ways; you'll also learn the 'secret' of how you can 'gain' WEALTH and all the good things that come with it.

These books will give you challenges and these books will give you promises. ALL YOU HAVE TO DO IS READ AND DO WHAT YOU WANT TO ABOUT IT. I'd like to hear about your journey. Won't you please write me and tell me how these books have helped you on your way? Let me know some of your dreams and rewards. Perhaps, I can share your achievements with others and, in return, reward you again. So, let me hear from you soon.

Suggested Reading

The following suggested reading list is offered as a self-improvement tool. As you complete reading each book, record the date.

Title	Date Started	Date Completed
The Quran		
Hill, Napoleon, *Think and Grow Rich*		
Chopra, Deepak, *The Seven Spiritual LAWS OF SUCCESS.*		
Robbins, Anthony, *UNLIMITED POWER*		
Allen, James, *AS THE MAN THINKETH*		
Bristol, Claude, *The Magic Of Believing.*		
Gibran, Kahlil, *The Profit*		
Clauson, George, *The Richest Man In Babylon*		
Conwell, Russell, *Acres of Diamonds*		
Mandino, Og, *The Greatest Salesman in the world.*		
Maltz, Maxwell, *Psycho-Cybernetics*		
Maslow, Abraham, *Motivation and personality*		
Peal, Norman, *The Power Of Positive Thinking.*		
Ziglar, Zig, *See You At The Top*		
Waitley, Dennis, *The Psychology of Winning.*		
Tozer, A.W. *The Pursuit of God.*		
Stone, W. Clement, *The Success System That Never Fails.*		
Sinetar, Marsha, *Do What You Love and The Money will Follow.*		
Schuller, Robert, *You can be the person you want to be.*		
Redfield, James, *CELESTINE PROPHECY*		
Danforth, William, *I DARE YOU*		
Rogers, Carl, *On becoming a person*		
Robert, Cavett, *Human Engineering & Motivation*		
Prather, H, *Notes to Myself*		
Peck, Scot, *The Road Less Traveled*		
Patent, Arnold, *YOU CAN HAVE IT ALL*		
Lazarus, Arnold, *In The Mind's Eye*		
Keyes, Ken, *Your Life Is A Gift*		
Jones, Charles, *Life is Tremendous*		
Jaafri, M, *The Mind-Conditioning System Part-Two*		
Hooper, D, *You Are What You Think*		
Harman, Bill, *GLOBAL MIND CHANGE*		
Goldratt, Eliyahu, *The Goal!*		
Gardner, John, *The Self-Renewal*		
Frankel, Victor, *Man's Search For Meaning*		
Jaafri, Mushtaq, *THE FIFTH MIND!*		
Dyer, Wayne, *The Sky's the Limit*		
DeVos, Rich, *BELIEVE*		
Corbin, Carolyn, *Strategies 2000*		
Copeland, K, *The Laws Of Prosperity*		
Carnegie, Dale, *How to win friends and influence people.*		
Butterworth, Eric, *Discover the power within you.*		
Bry, Adeleide, *Directing Movies of Mind*		
Brown, Barbara, *SUPERMINDS*		
Brande, Dorothhea, *Wake up and live*		
Blanchard, Ken, *The One Minute Manager*		
Bencon, Herb, *The Mind Body Effect*		
Anderson, U.S, *The Magic in your Mind!*		
Wright, John, *The Royal Road To Riches*		
Powers, Melvin, *How To Get Rich In Mail Order*		
Jaafri, Mushtaq, *Working Principles Of The Human Mind*		

About The Author

Mushtaq H. Jaafri, author, publisher, business consultant, teacher, and an Entrepreneur. He is the founder of The Mind-Conditioning Society, an organization devoted exclusively to the teaching of the working principles of the human Mind. He specializes in teaching sales, motivation, management, and communication skills and concepts to sales professionals. He has been in sales and management for more than 20 years. The Seven Spiritual Laws Of Nature is the result of his twenty five years of study, testing, research and practice. His current work with the public includes, lectures, seminars, conducts lectures and seminars on The Mind-Conditioning Techniques using a unique new system of 'thought' control.

Mr. Jaafri's current and long range professional goals are to establish a scientific laboratory where people from all over the world come to attend sessions in "Sitting for Creative Ideas". He is known as a teacher and a counselor and has been in the Self-Help and motivational fields since 1980. He has taught courses on Salesmanship, Goal-Setting, Positive Mental Attitude. He is the author of numerous books, including seven volume lecture notes on the LAWS OF NATURE philosophy, which were submitted in partial fulfillment of the requirements for the Degree of Doctor of Metaphysical Science in the Department Of Graduate Studies of the University of Metaphysics in Los Angeles, California. The doctoral degree Thesis was approved by the Examining Committee for the Thesis requirement for the Doctor of Metaphysical Science Degree of the University of Metaphysics. He is also the author of two part books, The Mind-Conditioning System, using the world's first <u>COMPUTER-LIKE</u> flow chart concept, using a cutting-edge technology.

Mushtaq H. Jaafri's ground-breaking work on The Seven Spiritual Laws of Nature has been honored in the world's prestigious publication, WHO'S WHO IN METAPHYSICS!

For twenty five years, he searched for something that would help people get beyond "Self-Limiting", negative 'thoughts' and EMOTIONS, and what could we do to release "Stress", achieve success, enjoy life and empower ourselves with a positive "State-Of-Mind". He found the answer in a world's first <u>COMPUTER-LIKE</u> flow chart using a cutting-edge technology.

His new book blends Eastern wisdom and cutting-edge Western Science, The physical and the Spiritual, with astounding accurate results. Dr. Jaafri has been residing in California for the last 30 years. He lives with his wife, Abida, and three sons, Mustafa, Murtaza and Mujtaba, in San Dimas, California, 91773 U.S.A.

Dr. Jaafri offers us all a unique, new, revelatory, and ultimately joyful vision of our true spirituality. One that could change your own life. And, perhaps the world.

If you are interested in having Dr. Mushtaq H. Jaafri speak to your group or organization, or wish to receive more information about The International Mind-Conditioning Society, or help us in any way to 'set' the new cultural transformation in motion during the next millennium, please do not hesitate to write me personally:

Dr. Mushtaq H. Jaafri
919 Sonora Ct.
San Dimas, CA 91773
U.S.A.

Dr. Mushtaq H. Jaafri

Current work with the public:
Lectures, seminars, conduct lectures and seminars on mind-conditioning techniques using a unique new system of thought control.

Current and long range professional goals:
To establish a scientific laboratory where people from all over the world come to attend sessions in "Sitting in Creatie Ideas".

Professional description:
Teacher, counselor.

Time in professional metaphysical practice:
Since 1980.

Schools:
University of Metaphysics, Doctoral Degree; Mind-Power Dynamics, "System Livings Diploma"; Life Dynamics Fellowship, Alphanetics Diploma.

Membership in:
Life Dynamics Fellowship.

Studied with:
Dr. Paul L. Masters.

Has taught and counseled the public in:
Taught courses on Salemanship, Goal-Setting, Positive Mental Attitude.

Professional metaphysical accomplishments:
Founded an international Mind-Conditioning Society, an organization devoted exclusively to the teachings of the working principles of the human mind; wrote a book "Laws of Nature".

Communications Address:
919 Sonora Ct.
San Dimas, CA 91773

The Faces of Mail Order

Your photo and a description of your business can be in this column! Send us a color or black & white photo of yourself along with a 50 word description of your business. Photo must be included for this free write-up. Send photo (non-returnable) and 50 words to: USA, P.O. Box 64, South Holland, IL 60473. Write: "USA has my permission to use my photo in its publications" on the back of your picture and sign the back of the photo as well.

Spencer & Debbie Judd
Optimal Telecom Reps.
2330 Janet Ct.
Anderson, IN 46012
Are getting their share of the 200 billion yr. In telecommunications business by GIVING AWAY FREE LONG DISTANCE! IF you're tired of the hype, and have $495 to start a REAL home based business, give them a call at: 1-800-688-1132.

MUSHTAQ H. JAAFRI
Author, Counselor, Entrepreneur, Publisher, Teacher:
919 Sonora Ct.
San Dimas, California 91773 U.S.A.
Mushtaq H. Jaafri, with over 25 years marketing experience has provided consultation services to MLM, Mail Order, Direct Sales companies and Distributor Organizations for the past seventeen years. He has also been active as a Distributor & has developed several independent income streams that keep him busy from 7am to 11pm most days. He maintains a working database of top level Self-Publishing and Marketing Companies including top-notch marketing professionals. MUSHTAQ JAAFRI WILL SEND YOU A FREE, 86-PAGE REPORT CALLED, "FORTUNE FROM YOUR MIND", WITH FULL REPRINT/RESALE RIGHTS. PLEASE CALL (1) (909) 599-0173 or simply write for FREE details to address above. USA Phone/Voicemail 1-909-599-0173

Marcella & Tracy Sutherland
Trends, Inc.
Innovative Products
& Services
721 Wing Ave.
Owensboro, KY. 42303
We promote Marketer's Advantage, a free distributorship that offers many benefits such as discounted printing and advertising, high impact envelopes, Internet and FOD services, mailing lists and much more. Respond now and also receive information on our nutritional products, super reports, and pager absolutely free. Please include SASE.

Review Of Literature

Unconsciously, I have been organizing this philosophy of personal self-development for the last twenty five years, not knowing that the research was intended for the birth of The Seven Spiritual Laws Of Nature.

I spent about 20+ years investigating this particular philosophy of individual achievement by utilizing certain laws of nature. And — then, I spent nearly 5 more years reviewing various literatures on the lives and accomplishments of some of the greatest as well as just average people of the world in all walks of life who actually utilized these LAWS OF NATURE, in one form or another, either knowingly or consciously or unconsciously. The purpose of my 5 years review type research was to cross-reference the main themes in the seven spiritual laws of nature, with things I had researched to support my own ideas.

The object of this research then, is to present my unique contribution of my own ideas to the existing field of philosophy and metaphysical science. the ideas presented in these seven spiritual laws of nature are NOT standard text filled with pages of theory but, down to earth facts based on the studies of the lives of hundreds of America's most successful people in all walks of life.

I was amazed and delighted to discover that practically every individual I studied knew of these spiritual laws of nature, although; some called these laws as principles or 'secrets'.

More information is available from the author on the ideas brought forth in this book. You may subscribe to a quarterly newsletter (to which readers may contribute), which chronicles these seven spiritual laws of nature, author's present experience and reflections on the upcoming cultural transformation movement.

In the quarterly newsletter, the author shall share the stories of people both great and just average individuals who are living proof of the soundness of these seven spiritual laws of nature.

Ahmad Bay Story

Ahmad Bay was trained in the Coptic Mystery School of Egypt. He came to the United States of America, so that his unique mental powers could be investigated by the United States Scientists.

The following is a direct quote from the U.S. Government publication, "CURRENT RESEARCH ON SLEEP AND DREAMS".
"By applying certain Mind-Power, Ahmad Bay had learned to 'know' himself to the degree, where certain ELEMENTS of the SUPER-CONSCIOUS or "GOD-CONSCIOUS" became CONSCIOUS with him thus, they became a part of his actions of every day life.
He had full control over his own breathing, pulse, heart beats and the flow of blood in his body.
To demonstrate his unique mental powers, he permitted the 'flesh' or tissues of the body to be pierced with long pins and daggers, seemingly without any pain. He either permitted the blood to flow or refused it to flow. However; his demonstration of body cataplesy was the most remarkable of all.
His body became rigged, the pulse almost imperceptible and respiration apparently ceased entirely. Consciousness was said to obliterate, and NOTHING was remembered of time spent in that state. In this mental state, Ahmad Bay permitted himself to be buried 'alive', underground with or without "coffin".

Now — listen to what Ahmad Bay says of himself:
"By many scientists and students, I am considered to be an unusual and super person. I am a very ordinary person, my ability, unusual as it may be, is entirely the result of the application of certain nature's laws, through the working of the human MIND."

I, as an author, am not suggesting that the goal is to do these things, and I am sure Ahmad Bay, meant them to be seen ONLY as a demonstration of what is possible but, IF, these possibilities are extended into the areas of our own health for an example, or the health of others, then imagine the increase we will experience in our lives.

In my quarterly newsletter, I shall share these exceptional stories.

Final Words!!

It is another nature's law that only a HABIT can subdue another Habit. So — in order for these written words to perform their chosen task, you must DISCIPLINE yourself with the FIRST of your NEW HABITS which is as follows:
READ THE ENTIRE, EACH SPIRITUAL LAW OF NATURE FOR THE NEXT SEVEN DAYS IN THIS PRESCRIBED MANNER, BEFORE YOU PROCEED TO THE NEXT LAW. Read the entire spiritual law aloud — if possible — once every night until you become thoroughly convinced that the principle of each spiritual law is sound, that it will accomplish for YOU that has been claimed for it.

As you read, (this is important) UNDERSCORE WITH PENCIL EVERY SENTENCE WHICH IMPRESSES YOU FAVORABLY! You continue in this manner until you have literally 'lived' with each spiritual law for seven days — and your reading has become a HABIT. My research and study during these twenty five years while putting this philosophy of individual together, revealed, without any room for doubt, that this whole universe revolves around the dance of number seven. There are seven days. There are seven skies. There seven spiritual laws, or principles or secrets in the nature.

And, what will be accomplished with this new HABIT?
Here in lies the 'hidden' SECRET of your future great accomplishments. As YOU repeat the WORDS of each spiritual LAW daily, they'll soon become a part of your conscious MIND but; more importantly, they will 'seep' into your inner-most level of the MIND, that

mysterious source which never sleeps, which creates your dreams, and often makes you ACT in a way you do not comprehend. This new HABIT will let you 'experience' the new YOU — and will let you 'assume' or feel your true Self (God-Self) and allows you to see through your physical body your own true spiritual individuality.

It shall also reveal a 'miracle' which contains a PASSWORD capable of making you FREE from your own self-made cocoon, which has imprisoned you for so long, and help you appropriate the great riches of life such as peace-of-mind, vibrant health and total financial prosperity.

In the seven spiritual laws of nature, I describe the virtues and the associated laws or principles that have helped me personally and countless others who have tried them to achieve spiritual satisfaction and material success.

I'm now writing to invite you to join me, and potentially thousands of others like you worldwide, in The International Mind-Conditioning Society, which will be based on the daily practice of these powerful seven spiritual laws of nature.

Participation in The Mind-Conditioning Society is open to anyone who chooses to put The seven spiritual laws of nature into effect by making a commitment to 'live' with each spiritual law of nature for seven days. Groups of friends or associates across the world can focus on one law together for seven days. I suggest starting a study group of family, friends, or co-workers where members meet once a week to discuss their experiences with the spiritual laws if the experience are dramatic, I invite you to write them down and mail them to me.

Having your attention on a spiritual law for seven days will completely transform your life, as it has mine, and if we collectively put our attention on the very same law of nature for seven days, we could soon reach a critical mass of successful people that could transform life on planet earth.

When enough people practice these seven spiritual laws of nature AT THE VERY SAME TIME (night and day), that is when our cultural transformation will surely begin to 'shift'. Then, the entire culture will begin to take these seven spiritual laws of nature seriously.

I believe that during this new millennium, more and more people will become conscious of these seven spiritual laws of nature, how else can I explain spiritual verses of the holy Quran, which is one of the four holy books sent by GOD. The holy Quran is the holy book of Is-lam. Is-lam is the religious faith of Muslims. My attention here, is only to introduce the readers, to facts I have found during my twenty five years — and none others.

Lest I be misunderstood, I wish here to state most emphatically that the spiritual transformation that I predict will NOT necessarily be religious in nature, instead, it will be somewhat spiritual in nature. People will relate to these seven spiritual laws of nature and NOT just the scientific laws or principles. People will enjoy a universal bond with each other, do less and accomplish more. When these seven spiritual laws of nature are incorporated into our consciousness, we will be empowered to create unlimited wealth with effortless ease. And, we will experience success in every endeavor, because these are the SAME (the VERY same) laws, nature uses to create everything in material existence.

To join The International Mind-Conditioning Society, all you need to do is send in your name, address to:

Dr. Mushtaq H. Jaafri
919 Sonora Ct.
San Dimas, California 91773
U.S.A

I'll personally send you all the details as the society develops. The establishment of The Mind-Conditioning Society actually represents the fulfillment of my own cherished dreams, which is to establish a scientific laboratory where people from all over the world come to attend sessions in "Sitting for Creative Ideas". This way, by helping me achieve my desire, will in turn, help you achieve spiritual success and the fulfillment of your desires. I can wish you no greater blessing.

With love and best regards,

Dr. Mushtaq H. Jaafri

Touched By An Angel

I earnestly believe that this amazing new book will not be complete, without sharing one of my most cherished moments in my entire life. This is the first time that I have had the courage to mention this. Heretofore, I have remained quiet on the subject, because I know, from my own attitude in connection with such matters, that I would be misunderstood, if I describe my unusual experience.

I have been emboldened now to reduce my experience to the printed page, because I am now less concerned about what "they say" than I was in the years that have passed.

This incidence I want to share with you happened back in the fall of 1980, when I had regular sessions in "sitting for creative ideas", for helping me put this message together for this book. Every night, over a long period of years, I held an imaginary council meeting with my own true Self, the God-Self!

The procedure was this, just before going to sleep at night, when all my family was asleep, I would go to my 'closet' upstairs, next to my younger son's room, where I would be undisturbed and alone. I would sit quietly for about 15 minutes trying to relax myself. I would have a few burning incenses in the closet where I sat in a chair. A fragrant odor and it's smoke instantly put my MIND in a state of mystical absorption.

Then, I would shut my eyes, and see, in my imagination, the presence of higher spiritual powers around me, while I held an imaginary council meeting with this higher power.

Here I had not only an opportunity to sit with the greater power in my own imaginations, but I actually dominated the council meeting, by having a "heart-to-heart" talk with my creator.

My purpose was to rebuild my own character, so I would represent God's thoughts.

Realizing, as I did, early in life, that I had to overcome the handicap of birth in an environment of fear, hate, jealousy, superstition, greed, revenge and anger.

I deliberately assign myself the task of voluntary rebirth through the council meeting I have described above.

My meeting of addressing to my creator (GOD) would vary, according to the need for help and guidance I was seeking, at the moment. I was astounded by the discovery that these imaginary council meetings had become apparently real.

One night, about quarter pass midnight, as I was indulging my imagination through these nightly meetings, I vividly saw, what appeared to be an angel, sitting in a corner, writing something in a golden book. In my own imagination, I asked the angel, "What are you writing about"?

The angel replied, "He was writing the names of all those people whom God loves the most".

I asked the angel, "Is my name listed in that golden book"?

The angel looked and looked from the first page of that golden book to the last page of the book, and said, "NO"!

The angel repeated his answer by saying that, "My name was NOT mentioned anywhere in the golden book."

I then, asked the angel, "please write down my name in the list of those people who loved the MANKIND or humanity the most." He said that he would, and he did write down my name among the people on the list who also loved the MAN-KIND the most, and then suddenly the angel vanished.

Having seen the angel face-to-face, and being in that brilliant, bright, glowing white light, I observed that while having this imaginary meeting with the angel, I was lifted to a high level of mental stimulation.

It was indeed, a "state-of-mind", that I cannot fully describe in one volume book.

Being touched by an angel, instantly put me in a positive "state-of-mind", where I experienced the sensation of being in control of my own Mind and Body. The conversation that took place between myself and the angel purely through my own MIND, was an experience where I could feel or 'assume' my other Self the God Self, and I could truly see through my physical body, my own true spiritual individuality.

During my twenty five years of research and studies while putting the manuscript of this book together, I also witnessed a scripture quotation from the parallel Bible, in the book of Revelation 20:15, and I quote:

"AND WHOSOEVER WAS NOT FOUND
WRITTEN IN THE BOOK OF LIFE
WAS CAST INTO THE LAKE OF FIRE."

Most of my life I truly believed that the whole purpose of life is to serve MAN-KIND or humanity, and when we choose actions that brings happiness and success to others, that is when we achieve true greatness, success and everything that comes with it.

A few days later, as I was indulging my imagination in my nightly meetings, I saw the very same angel again.

This time, he was sitting quietly, with his wings gently beating and his left hand on the first page of that golden book. The angel seemed to be pondering on something as he gazed at the sky. I was curious to learn what was going on, so I walked toward the angel and looked over his shoulders.

As I gazed at the golden book, to my amazement, I saw my name written on top of the page among the list of people whom GOD regard with favor.

PEACE!

P.S. These meetings became so realistic that I became fearful of their consequences, and discontinued them for several years. This experience was so uncanny, I was afraid if I continued them I would lose sight of the fact that the meetings were purely experiences of my imagination.

This is the first time that I have had the courage to mention this incidence. I'm sharing this only to show what is possible, when you do the mental exercises using the <u>COMPUTER-LIKE</u> flow charts using the cutting-edge technology for success.

If you too, have had any encounters with the higher powers or ever touched by an angel, I would love to hear from you. Perhaps, we could share your experiences with other member of our society.

This information that follows is meant only to be seen to demonstrate what is possible, "If you truly believe in the fulfillment of your dream and persist!"

January 19, 1998

Mr. Mushtaq Jaafri
919 Sonora Ct.
San Dimas, CA 91773

Dear Mr. Jaafri,

This is just a brief note to check with you regarding your plans for the publication of your book, The Seven Spiritual Laws of Nature.

We are now preparing our production schedule for the next three months, and I do hope that we shall have the pleasure of working with you on your project in the near future.

If you have any questions about specifics in our contract, or our payment terms, do not hesitate to contact me, toll free, at 1(800)873-2003.

I would appreciate hearing from you soon.

Sincerely,

Johnnye C. Bradley
Director of Publishing

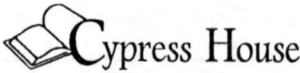
Cypress House

155 Cypress Street · Fort Bragg, California 95437 · (707) 964-9520 · Fax (707) 964-7531

January 8, 1998

Mr. Mushtaq H Jaafri
919 Sonora Court
San Dimas, CA 91773

Dear Mr. Jaafri,

    Thank you for choosing to use our services..

    Your manuscript has been scheduled for an evaluation and, since we are quite busy at this time, it will most likely take the maximum six weeks. You should be receiving the evaluation the week of February 19th. If that timeline changes, we'll be sure to let you know.

Once again thanks for choosing our sevices. If you have any questions please give us a call or drop us a line.

All the best,

Pradha Bush

Pradha Bush
Office Manager

http://www.cypresshouse.com   email: publishing@cypresshouse.com   SAN: 297-9004

MORRIS PUBLISHING

1-12-98

Mushtaq Jaafri
919 Sonora Ct.
San Dimas, CA 91773

Mr. Jaafri:

I received your letter and questions, along with pages 119-124 and the revised mail order page.

To answer your questions:
1. Yes, you will be charged for the actual page count--150 to 160 pages is the best estimate I can offer at this time. It may be a few pages more with the addition of the seven pages recently submitted.
2. Regarding production time, if all of your materials are received by Jan, 19, 1998, then
 - a typeset book requires 45 to 60 working days which would make your due dates March 23 to April 13.
 - a camera-ready book requires 35 to 45 working days which would make your due dates March 9 to March 23.
We briefly discussed submitting your book camera-ready--I believe you were going to speak with the gentleman that typeset your book originally and see if he could easily reformat it to the 5 1/2 by 8 1/2 size. This would save you time, money and allow you to place the flow charts within the text as you would like. If we typeset your book, they will have to be placed at the end of the chapters that they occur in. I'm sorry we have this limitation.
3. Yes, we could set up the logo and use it on the title page, copyright page, back cover, or wherever you ask us to use it.
4. Yes, your cover can be designed in full color. There are additional costs for designing and printing a full color cover and they have been included in the previous quotes. Our art director will discuss your cover design more thoroughly when we are ready to begin working on your manuscript.
5. Yes, the mail order page can be placed before the certificates and letters. However, it would be easier for the reader to find if it were the last page of the book. You may want to reconsider the placement of this page. You can see on page 42 in the Publishing Guide that our borders are all quite simple. Would you like to choose one of these or is any border needed for your mail order page?
6. Yes, you do need to complete a mail order page. I'v enclosed one for you.
7. Yes, you will receive proofs of both the text and the cover.
8. We live in a Mac world here, but you could submit text files saved as ASCII on an IBM disk. We'll still have to format the text so it will be priced as a typeset book ($5/pg).

Whew! I think I came up with answers for your questions, but if I missed any, please let me know. I look forward to hearing from you soon.

Sincerely,

Kirsten

Kirsten Bespalec
Manager

3212 E. Hwy. 30 • Kearney, NE 68847 • 800-650-7888 • Fax 308-237-0263

Rutledge Books, Inc.

Box 315, 8 F.J. Clarke Circle Bethel, CT 06801-0315
(800) 2RUTLEDGE (800) 278-8533 Local: (203) 778-5925 Fax: (800) 962-8345

December 3, 1997

M. Jaafri
919 Sonora Court
San Dimas, CA 91773

Dear M. Jaafri:

Thank you for your interest in Rutledge Books' publishing program. We exist to serve authors such as you. We seek those who have something to say, and know how to say it.

Enclosed you will find a copy of our brochure explaining our editing, designing, publishing, promotion, and distribution plan. I'm sure you will find the information both interesting and relevant.

To start the process, simply send us a copy of your completed manuscript for review. There is no cost or obligation.

Our editors will read your work and determine its suitability for production. If your book is accepted, we will also include a proposal outlining the details and costs involved in publication. In addition, you will receive a free copy of one of our previously published books so that you may examine the quality of Rutledge's workmanship for yourself.

Of course, if your book is not accepted for publication we will notify you and we can make arrangements for the return of your manuscript, if you so desire.

For your convenience, we have enclosed a postage-paid, self-addressed Priority Mail envelope for your use. If you have any questions, please write or call me personally. Please note our new street address is: 107 Mill Plain Rd., Danbury, CT 06810; and our new fax number is: (203) 798-7272.

Sincerely,

Merrilee Warholak

Merrilee Warholak
Acquisitions Editor

Rutledge Books, Inc.
107 Mill Plain Road, Danbury, CT 06811

203·778·5925 ♦ 203·798·7272 (FAX)

Authors' Hotline: 800·2·RUTLEDGE (800·278·8533)
www.rutledgebooks.com ♦ info@rutledgebooks.com

December 22, 1997

Dr. Mustaq Jaafri
919 Sonora Court
San Dimas, CA 91773

Dear Dr. Jaafri,

We were pleased to receive your manuscript. Already, our editorial staff has scheduled *The Seven Spiritual Laws of Nature* for reading and review. A report, which will apprise you of your manuscript's potential for publication, will be mailed to you within a few weeks' time.

You will also receive, free of charge, a published Rutledge title for your examination. We are sure you will appreciate the attractive style and quality production of our books. Your manuscript would be crafted with the same care and high standards. In addition, we will design a varied plan of publicity and promotion.

If your manuscript is accepted for publication, when we mail our editorial report, we will include an Agreement spelling out the details of our plan, including the cost and easy payment schedule.

We hope to soon have the pleasure of adding you to the Rutledge family of authors. In the meantime, if you have any questions, please contact us.

Sincerely,

David Villegas
Acquisitions Department

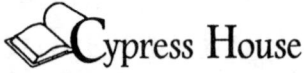
Cypress House

155 Cypress Street • Fort Bragg, California 95437 • (707) 964-9520 • Fax (707) 964-7531

November 25, 1997

Jeff Jaafri
919 Sonora
San Dimas, CA 91773-1488

Dear Mr. Jaafri,

Thank you for asking about our publishing services. For the past twelve years we have provided editorial, design, production and marketing services to some of the most successful independent publishers in the U.S. Most of our business is repeat business, not only because of the quality of our work, but because we depend on repeat business we pay special attention to our clients. Since we're independent publishers ourselves, we know how important it is to have a quality product at a good price, delivered on time. We stand behind the titles we produce, and we have the contacts to promote and market your books nationwide and worldwide.

The enclosed brochure will answer many of your questions. Since every book is unique, we'll need to know more about your book and your goals before providing prices. Please fax or mail the enclosed worksheet, noting any special requirements you might have, and we'll calculate how much it will cost to publish your book. If you're uncertain about options, please call us and we'll be happy to offer suggestions.

If you haven't prepared a marketing plan or had your book professionally critiqued, we offer a thorough and professional evaluation for $150. We'll provide a detailed, multi-page analysis of your book's content, structure and sales potential that will save you time and money while pinpointing possible problem areas. If you'd like to take advantage of this offer, please send your manuscript and payment (along with return postage), allowing 4-6 weeks for our report.

If you're new to self-publishing, you'll find the enclosed Recommended Reading List helpful. You can purchase these books from your local bookstore, but if you order from us, I'll enclose a book we've published as a gift. It will speak more about the quality of our work than any words I write.

You can support independent publishing by ordering one or more titles from the enclosed catalog. We've edited, designed or published these books, and your title can be included in the next issue.

Thanks for contacting us. We look forward to working with you.

Sincerely,

John Fremont
John Fremont
Senior Editor

http://www.cypresshouse.com   email: publishing@cypresshouse.com   SAN: 297-9004

DORRANCE
PUBLISHING CO.
INC.

643 Smithfield Street • Pittsburgh, PA 15222 • (412) 288-4543 • FAX (412) 288-1786

November 6, 1997

Dr. Mushtaq H. Jaafri
919 Sonora Ct
San Dimas, CA 91773

Dear Dr. Jaafri:

We wanted to let you know that we have received your work, "The Seven Spiritual Laws of Nature: A Practical Guide to the Fulfillment...", and look forward to reading it.

We have enclosed our Author's Pre-Publishing Data questionnaire, as well as other materials for your information. Please complete the questionnaire and return it to us in the envelope provided within 7 days. This information will be helpful to us as we proceed with our review and production analysis of the manuscript you have submitted for subsidy publication.

We plan to get back to you as soon as possible regarding your work. In the meantime, please feel free to call or write to James C. Dunlap at 800-398-7654 if you have any questions.

Sincerely,

Amy Woodall
Proposal Services Manager

P.S. Should you wish us to return your manuscript, in the case that we do not publish your work, please send a self-addressed, stamped envelope appropriate to the size of your material at this time so we can place it in your file or upon requesting your manuscript's return. Thank you.

May 19, 1997

Jeff Jaafry
919 Sonora
San Dimas, CA 91773

Dear Jeff:

You have been waiting so patiently—and the time has *finally* come! We have nailed down a date for the seminar you called about: Tuesday, June 24th at 5:30pm. That's when you will learn all about the possibilities of creating your own radio program on KYPA, Personal Achievement Radio. You can be on the air in Los Angeles—America's second largest radio market!

Seating is limited, so make sure you reserve your spot as soon as possible. Only those who RSVP will be admitted. Just call our receptionist Jenny at 310-289-7799. She is waiting to hear from you. And we're looking forward to seeing you soon.

Sincerely,

Charles Andrew Whatley
General Sales Manager

W. DOUGLAS POMROY
1625 East 46th Street
Odessa, Texas 79762

July 24, 1996

Mushtaq H. Jaafri

919 Sonora CT.

San Dimas, CA 91773

Dear Jeff,

    Please send your special package right away. Not unlike yourself, I too have searched for the elusive "secret," for years.

    I have probably read over 500 books, and purchased over 200, on success, business, MLM and similar information. In addition, I have also had dealings with W. Clement Stone, via his magazine. And Napoleon Hills cassette program "The Science of Achievement."

    Whatever this one step is, I have yet to find it and put it to use. I am looking forward to seeing your approach and putting it to work.

    I have enclosed a check for $4.95 according to your letter. Thank you for your time.

Sincerely,

Douglas

Douglas

GABRIEL TUDOSE
BOOKS-REPORTS
109, FALCONER ST. SUITE 3
NO. TONAWANDA NY 14120

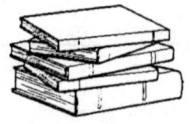

March 24, 1997

Dear Mr. Jaafri,

Several weeks ago I received from the following reports:

"The Mind-Conditioning System"
"70 Money-Making Reports"

I didn't receive from you the writen rights to sell these reports.Please,help me,and send me the authorization to sell these reports.Thank you!

Sincerely,
Gabriel Tudose
Gabriel Tudose

P.S. "The Mind-Conditioning System" is amazing.Thank you!

PENNCORP FINANCIAL, INC.

EXECUTIVE OFFICES: 1001 WADE AVENUE, RALEIGH, NORTH CAROLINA 27605 • 919-834-0751

April 2, 1993

Jeff Jaafri
Sunbelt Region
National Executive Fund Life Insurance Company
7041 Owensmouth Ave., #204-205
Canoga Park, CA 91303

Dear Jeff:

I am very pleased to inform you that you are a member of the 1993 National President's Club, our Company's most prestigious group of producers. The qualification for this year's President's Club was competitive, and your outstanding efforts place you in an elite category.

PennCorp would like to recognize your talent and perseverance at the 1993 National President's Club gathering at the El San Juan Resort in Puerto Rico. The President's Club deserves only the best, and we believe you will be highly pleased with the luxurious tropical setting that awaits you.

It is the commitment and effort by you and others like you that make our Company successful. It is an honor to work with such a talented and dedicated individual. I look forward to seeing you in San Juan.

Sincerely,

David J. Stone

123 NORTH WACKER DRIVE • CHICAGO, ILLINOIS 60606

September 18, 1991

Jeff Jaafri
919 Sonora Ct.
San Dimas, CA 91773

Dear Jeff:

CONGRATULATIONS on completing "The Key to Personal Self-Development Program". You have achieved a significant level of development which will serve you for many years to come. The right attitude and activities will always help you achieve your personal as well as career goals. I know you will display your achievement proudly which is endorsed by our President, Richard Ravin and our Chairman and Founder, W. Clement Stone.

Your certificate and emblem will be presented to you at an appropriate Regional function by your Regional Manager.

Congratulations again.

Best regards,

John Hardy
Vice President and Director of Training
7th Essential North American Organization

JH\fb

Enclosures

cc: Lee Brown, Lou Schiffman

EAGLE STAR
INTERNATIONAL FINANCIAL SERVICES

MEMORANDUM

To   :   All Field Force and Managers
From   :   Mahmoud Nodjoumi
Date   :   8/7/90

Subj   :   PERSONAL SUCCESS PLAN SEMINAR

Dr. Jaafri is conducting "The Million Dollar Personal Success Plan" seminar based on Napoleon Hill's famous 13 principles of success.

I am inviting all those interested in acquiring a blueprint for success to attend this seminar, an introductory session will be conducted on Monday 23/7/90 at 7 pm sharp in our training room 605.

Everyone is invited to attend this special introductory seminar but because of the limited class room space available only the first 25 to 30 persons will be accommodated.

If you are interested, please register your name with Pamela Vasandani so that we can prepare your work sheets and hand-outs well in advance.

Deadline for registration is Monday, 16/7/90.

Regards,

Mahmoud Nodjoumi
Managing Director

c.c.   A. Vickers
        D. Sherman
        P. Vasandani

DR. CHARLES E. LETTIN
Doctor of Metaphysical Sciences
5304 Clark St.   Box 508
KEYES, CA 95328

3-1-88

DR. M. JAAFRI

I AM AMAZED AT YOUR WORK. WHAT I HAVE STUDIED SO FAR IS PERFECT. AM LOOKING FORWARD TO COMPLETING EACH & EVERY LESSON.

HOW YOU COULD HAVE ALL THAT WORK PRINTED SO NEATLY - SO ATTRACTIVE & FOR SO LITTLE ($25.00) IS ALSO AMAZING--

WILL KEEP IN TOUCH

Dr. Charles E. Lettin

THE PHILOSOPHICAL RESEARCH SOCIETY

Manly P. Hall, President and Founder   Patricia C. Ervin, Vice President

October 11, 1987

Dr. M. Jaafri
919 Sonora Ct.
San Dimas, CA 91773

Dear Dr. Jaafri:

    Thank you for the impressive package you sent us in regard to you and all your activities.

    The P.R.S does not open its doors to an outside organization and its teachings.

    What we can do is to invite you to speak at our Lyceum on a Friday morning from 10 to 11:30. This is for the purpose of our getting acquainted with you and your message, and no honorarium is paid to you. (The attendance is usually small). So while we cannot offer your course to the public, we can have you as a speaker. If you are interested in a Friday morning, please call me.

                                      Sincerely,

                                       (Mrs.) Pearl M. Thomas
                                       Librarian

3910 Los Feliz Boulevard, Los Angeles, California 90027-2399, Telephone (213) 663-2167

University of Metaphysics

THE UNIVERSITY OF METAPHYSICS IS A HIGHER EDUCATIONAL DIVISION OF THE
NATIONAL METAPHYSICS INSTITUTE

7801 HOLLYWOOD BLVD.
LOS ANGELES, CALIFORNIA 90046
(213) 874-4296 or 397-7044

May 19, 1983

Dear Dr. Jaafri:

Congratulations! Your Doctoral Thesis has been reviewed and found acceptable.

This effort has been your final step in meeting the Doctoral Degree requirements of the University of Metaphysics, and we are just as proud of you as you must be of yourself.

You will soon be receiving your Doctoral Degree to proudly display for the rest of your life.

We hope that you have enjoyed your Doctoral Degree Program and Ministerial Training, and that you will recommend the University of Metaphysics to others.

Let us know immediately when you have a change of address so that we can keep your personal student file up-to-date, which is <u>necessary</u> for your Ministerial status.

Again, congratulations, and May God Within You Grant You Life's Final Degree of Wisdom.

Sincerely,

Paul L. Mastorakos, Msc.D.
Dean/University of Metaphysics

PLM:ko

RONALD REAGAN

December 2, 1983

Dear Mr. Jaafri:

I feel you and I are in a special partnership together, a partnership dedicated to rebuilding our nation.

That is why it is such a privilege for me to present you with your new 1984 Sustaining Membership card, which is a symbol of our dedication to achieving the goals we share for America.

To a degree parallelled by few other Americans, you have directly helped me, my Administration and our Party bring about the most dramatic change in government policy in 50 years.

Without your financial support of the National Committee, I could not have taken the first critical and long-overdue steps to restore economic stability and strengthen our nation's security.

As a result of our major tax and spending cuts, people are going back to work and there is again hope and optimism in our country.

And thanks to our long-term commitment to rebuild and modernize our armed forces, we have let the world know that once again America will do what is necessary to protect our vital national interests.

Now I am hopeful you will help me complete our unfinished agenda for America by renewing your membership in our Party for 1984.

I am the first to recognize that if we lose the 1984 election to the Democrats, we will also lose, perhaps forever, the opportunity to carry to completion the programs that will ensure a better, more secure future for you and every American.

That's why your renewed financial commitment to the National Committee today is particularly critical. The Committee will be making absolutely indispensable direct cash expenditures of $6.4 million for our party's Presidential campaign after the National Convention in Dallas.

And above and beyond the key role the Committee will play in our Presidential effort, your membership renewal will help determine whether or not we can retain our Senate majority and increase our strength in the House of Representatives next year.

Paid for and authorized by the Republican National Committee

As I watch events unfold on Capitol Hill and listen to what our Democrat opponents say, I am convinced that the election of a liberal Democrat President would be a disaster for you, me and generations of Americans that will follow us.

Our opponents have already declared they want to repeal our tax cut and restore their billion dollar welfare spending programs. They have also said they will impose a one-sided "nuclear freeze" on our nation and slow down, if not stop, our national defense build-up which is so necessary to maintain world peace and our freedom.

The Democrats are making unjust and irresponsible attacks on us daily, falsely charging our cuts in wasteful spending programs have caused "misery" and "hardship" for our fellow citizens.

They are being supported by a well-financed coalition of special interest groups intent on restoring the taxpayer-funded giveaways that for years were the source of their income and political power.

To counter this liberal attempt to win back complete control of our government, the National Committee, which is spearheading our entire national campaign effort, has set a budget goal of $31.9 million for 1984, its largest election year budget ever.

This figure represents the minimum the Committee must raise to fund its entire range of campaign programs, including cash to candidates, national advertising and a variety of key support services for our Presidential, Senatorial, and Congressional campaigns.

But they can only raise this sum if you renew your Membership now. Truly, if members as dedicated as you fail to make a renewal contribution to the Committee, our entire effort will be in jeopardy.

I hope you will consider all that is at stake for our country when you sit down to write your check, and make every effort to increase your membership contribution for 1984.

We have worked too hard to repair the damage done by the last Democrat Administration to let them return to power and restore the same failed policies which brought America to the brink of economic collapse and strategic inferiority just three years ago.

Between now and the election I will devote every spare moment I can to taking our message of hope and optimism to the people, contrasting our record of achievement to the Democrats' proven record of failure.

But we cannot win this election without your help as an active 1984 Sustaining Member. I pray I can count on you to play an important role in completing our unfinished agenda and making our vision of a stronger, freer and more prosperous America a reality.

Sincerely,

Ronald Reagan

RR/sq

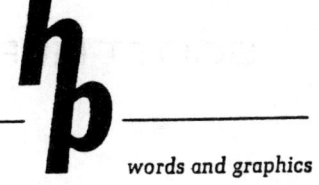

harold prince

words and graphics

August 25, 1979

Mr. M. Jaafri
International Mind-Conditioning Academy
919 Sonora Ct.
San Dimas, California 91773

Dear Mr. Jaafri:

After chatting briefly on the telephone with you the other day, I re-read your manuscript.

The contents are simply too important to be wasted. Yet, as your book is written, it is unpublishable.

I can't let that happen.

So what I've decided is this:

I'll handle your project, both as a literary consultant and as an agent -- <u>personally</u>.

That's how much the book affects me.

The attached summary of my services will tell you a bit more about me.

Read it.

Then read the letter of agreement that follows it.

Execute that letter, return it to me -- and we're in business.

Telephone, if you need further clarification.

Sincerely,

Harold Prince
212-879-2847

HP/dim

240 E. 76th STREET, NEW YORK 10036 ■ 233-5949

SCOTT MEREDITH

SCOTT
MEREDITH
LITERARY
AGENCY

October 12, 1983

Dear Dr. Jaafri:

Thanks very much for your latest inquiry of August 29th.

I'd like to compliment you on the determination you show in wanting your book THE LAWS OF NATURE in print. Writers as a breed are unusually determined to see their work published at all costs; but with you, Mr. Jaafri, determination goes a bit further. You truly believe that you have a message for the world and you are determined that the world shall have it. I think that's admirable.

You must note however, that unless you are 'positive' about the opinions expressed by our consideration report and substantially rework your manuscript, our opinion will inevitably remain the same.

We'd like nothing better than to see your work published.

845 THIRD AVENUE, NEW YORK, N.Y. 10022   TEL. (212) 245-5500
TELEX: FSFMELA 224705 · CABLES: SCOTTMERE
OFFICES AND AGENTS IN PRINCIPAL COUNTRIES

Prentice-Hall, Inc.
Englewood Cliffs, N.J. 07632

Telex No. 13-5423

July 20, 1979

Mr. M. Jaafri
International Mind-Conditioning Academy
919 Sonora Court
San Dimas, California 91773

Dear Mr. Jaafri:

Thank you for giving me the opportunity to consider your project on THE LAWS OF NATURE.

It seems to be an excellent contribution to its field. However, it does not fit into Prentice-Hall's current publishing program and I must decline any further interest in it. My suggestion is that you contact other companies who may be able to fit this type of publication into their plans.

I appreciate your sharing it with us and I wish you the best of success with it.

Sincerely,

John Isley
Editor - Psychology

JI:mc

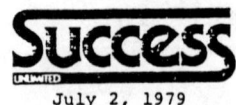

July 2, 1979

Mr. M. Jaafri
International Mind-Conditioning
   Academy
919 Sonora Ct.
San Dimas, CA 91773

Dear Mr. Jaafri,

Thank you very much for your recent letter explaining your interest in having your book <u>The Laws of Nature</u> published.

We are not regularly publishing books at this time. However, I would be interested in reading a sample chapter and outline of your book. We do not have the time or staff to consider a book-length manuscript, but if a sample showed enough promise, we could probably get geared up to do it.

Sincerely,

Robert C. Anderson
Editor

/by

SUCCESS UNLIMITED MAGAZINE 401 NORTH WABASH AVENUE CHICAGO, ILLINOIS 60611 PHONE 312 828-9500

Vantage Press, Inc.

BOOK PUBLISHERS • 6253 HOLLYWOOD BLVD. • HOLLYWOOD, CALIF. 90028 • TELEPHONE 213/465-8487

June 21, 1979

Mr. M. Jaafri
International Mind-Conditioning Academy
919 Sonora Court
San Dimas, CA   91773

Dear Mr. Jaafri:

Thank you for submitting your manuscript, THE LAWS OF NATURE. It was perused by my Hollywood staff with much interest, and we would certainly like to explore further the possibilities of publishing it under the Vantage imprint. However, I want to respond to your cover letter of June 18 immediately so that you can formulate your plans.

First of all, it is not possible to complete your book for the fall market of 1979. To set type and design this book would consume at least 8-10 months in production. Furthermore, even with a rough estimate of cost, I must advise you would have a publishing fee of more than $7,000. Please take note that this is a very rough estimate, and depending upon how the various illustrative and question and answer sections, etc., are treated, the production costs could vary greatly.

Not wanting to delay your program in getting this book on the market, I hasten to advise you regarding the above factors.

In the meantime, if you are interested in a concrete contract to publish your book with Vantage, please contact me immediately. Feel free to telephone my office collect, or write if you prefer. A postage-free envelope is enclosed for your convenience.

I look forward to your reply.

Cordially,

HERMAN RUSS
Vice President

HR/cr
enc.

MAIN OFFICE, 516 WEST 34TH STREET • NEW YORK, N.Y. 10001 • ESTABLISHED 1949

The Theosophical Publishing House

A Department of The Theosophical Society in America

publishers/importers

306 West Geneva Road
Post Office Box 270
Wheaton, Illinois 60187
Area Code 312/665-0123

19 July 1979

Mr. M. Jaafri
919 Sonora Court
San Dimas, California 91773

Dear Mr. Jaafri,

After giving your manuscript a thorough going-over here in the Editorial Department, I find that it is really not appropriate for a Quest book. Our books are all totally theosophical in nature regardless of the subject or format of each. For example, all of our literature on thought-forms, meditation on the virtues, developing the will, etc., are for self-illumination whereas one can read into your 'self-help' structure here an attitude for developing selfish ends. There is undoubtedly a market for such a book, but we are not it.

One of the most appropriate publishers for it may well be DeVorss who is in California. I have directed authors there in the past and some have been accepted. You might contact them first. Their address is P. O. Box 550 - Marina Del Rey, Calif. 90291.

I wish you much success with your book, which I am returning to you under separate cover.
All good wishes to you.

Sincerely,

Rosemarie Stewart
Senior Editor

W. CLEMENT & JESSIE V. STONE FOUNDATION

July 11, 1978

Dedicated to help make this a better world in which to live

Mr. Mushtaq H. Jaafri
919 Sonora Court
San Dimas, CA 91773

Dear Mr. Jaafri:

Mr. W. Clement Stone has asked that I respond to your letter and to congratulate you on demonstrating the principle that "in every adversity there are seeds of equal opportunity." It sounds as though you have seized that opportunity and are doing a fantastic job.

We wholeheartedly agree with you that the concepts of Mr. Stone and of Napoleon Hill need to be taught in schools and businesses. We are doing some of this in a program which we call the Achievement Motivation Program, which has been accepted in a number of schools, and through which we are using Mr. Stone's and Napoleon Hill's concepts. We have plans to integrate more of this teaching in our plans. At present, our challenge is to handle the many requests and inquiries which come to our office daily about what is being done now in this field.

We certainly cannot tell a man like yourself what he should do with his monies or his goal in life. We have been working through existing colleges, such as Trinity College in Deerfield, Illinois and Austin College in Sherman, Texas. At the University of Michigan in Ann Arbor, we have five Ph.D. theses that have been completed using Achievement Motivation principles.

On page 4 of your letter you have outlined some suggested approaches to your center, and state that you would like to share these with Mr. Stone at some time. Due to Mr. Stone's extremely busy schedule and personal commitments to his family, he has decided to limit meetings of this type and has asked people like myself to do first-steps of meeting and discussing these ideas. And so if you would care to outline some ideas of this type and forward them to me, I would be more than glad to respond or react to the ideas you have, and then inform Mr. Stone.

Again, we certainly want to congratulate you on your success and look forward to hearing from you. Keep up the good work!

Sincerely,

Lacy Hall

Lacy Hall, Ed.D.
Director
Achievement Motivation Program

LH/et

(Transcribed and signed in Dr. Hall's absence)

111 EAST WACKER DRIVE · Suite 510 · CHICAGO, ILLINOIS 60601 · Telephone (312) 565-1100

The President of
Columbia College
by authority vested in him by the Board of Trustees and upon recommendation of the faculty confers upon

Mishkin M. Kasfir

the degree of

Master of Arts

In Witness Whereof, this diploma is issued bearing the seal of the college

Given at Los Angeles, in the State of California

June 26, 1965

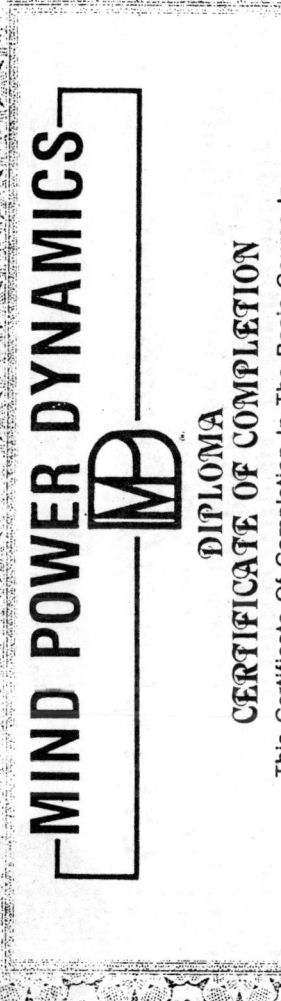

PRACTITIONERS DIPLOMA

NATIONAL METAPHYSICS INSTITUTE

TO WHOM THESE LETTERS SHALL COME
Having Successfully Passed The Required Examination

Mushtaq H. Jaafri

Has been awarded this certificate to professionally engage in the treatment of physical and mental ailments and conditions through the use of Spiritual Mind Treatment in the capacity of

Metaphysical Practitioner

In Witness whereof, we have hereunto affixed our hand and seal this 28th day of Mar, 1983 at Los Angeles, California

President
Secretary

University of Metaphysics

To All To Whom These Presents May Come, Greetings:

Having completed all Doctoral Requirements, The University of Metaphysics, a higher educational Division of the National Metaphysics Institute, Inc. Ministry

Does Hereby Confer On

M. Zaafri

The Degree OF

Doctor of Metaphysical Science

With all rights, privileges, and honors thereto as it pertains to their Ministerial affiliation with the National Metaphysics Institute. This diploma is thereby granted as evidence of Doctoral standing in the Ministry of this organization.

Awarded this 24th day of January, 1984

Lifetime Certificate Of Recognition

"WHO'S WHO IN METAPHYSICS"

This Is To Certify That

Dr. Mushtaq H. Jaafri

has received recognition for status in the field of professional metaphysics by having been recognized for publication in WHO'S WHO IN METAPHYSICS

In testimony, we, the publishers, herewith acknowledge this professional recognition in Beverly Hills, California

This 19th *day of* September, 19 85

FREE FORTUNE FROM YOUR MIND

LAWS OF NATURE

POWERFUL FORCES WITH-IN YOUR MIND CAN TURN YOUR EVERY DESIRE INTO WONDERFUL REALITY. Mystical, Motivational and inspiring NEW 5½ x 8½ perfect binding colorful book, "The Seven Spiritual **LAWS OF NATURE**", is an extraordinary MIND-CONDITIONING program that shows you "How to quickly, easily and effortlessly take control of your own life. **BASED ON SEVEN NATURAL LAWS,** which govern all of creation, this NEW book transform lives with cutting-edge technology. VIRTUALLY NOTHING CAN HOLD YOU BACK, ONCE YOU FULLY UNDERSTAND YOUR OWN TRUE NATURE. **WORLD'S FIRST COMPUTER-LIKE** flow charts reveal amazing **'secrets'** and magical methods that instantly release stress, tension, nervousness. Experience amazing new inner-peace, self-confidence and vibrant health. RESULTS GUARANTEED. **ONLY $14** (Refundable). Package includes **a FREE 14-Page guide, "How to Make a fortune selling Information by Mail"** ... plus FREE BOOK SELLING DISTRIBUTORSHIP - TWO PLANS - **1000%** Profit - 596 titles, with FULL RE-PRINT/RE-SELL rights. SEND Two First Class U.S Postage Stamps for FREE details ONLY.

** MAIL $14 CHECK OR M.O. FOR BOOK PACKAGE **

MUSHTAQ H. JAAFRI   Dept. _____
919 SONORA CT.
SAN DIMAS, CA 91773

Satisfaction 100% Guaranteed.

To order additonal copies of **The Seven Spiritual Laws of Nature**, please complete the information below.

Ship to: (please print)

    Name _____

    Address _____

    City, State, Zip _____

    Day phone _____

___ copies of *The Laws Of Nature* @ $14.00 each $ _____

Postage and handling @ $1.00 per book $ _____

CA residents add 8.5% sales tax $ _____

Total amount enclosed $ _____

Please make checks payable to: **Mushtaq H. Jaafri**

    Send to: **Mushtaq H. Jaafri**
                      919 Sonora Ct.
                      San Dimas, CA 91773

***** Free Bonus Offer If You Act Know *****

Free Camera-ready 8½ x 11 Flow Charts for both Negative & Positive Emotions — plus, free dynamic report "THE MILLION DOLLAR PERSONAL SUCCESS PLAN". This amazing report reveals a five-point success 'essentials' plan that shows you how to develop "earth-shaking" self-motivation, avoid discouragements and frustration and much much more.

Free information about the business opportunity for selling information by mail order for huge profits. Thousands of reports. Free reprint resell rights to every one item!!!

Be sure to mail this mail order page with your order for Free Bonus.

EDUCATIONAL CONSULTANT IS READY TO ASSIST, EDUCATE, AND TRAIN YOU IN THE TECHNIQUES AND PRACTICES OF MIND POWER DYNAMICS

If you are interested in having Dr. Mushtaq H. Jaafri speak to your group or organization, or wish to receive more information about The International Mind-Conditioning Society, or help us in any way to 'set' the new cultural transformation in motion during the next millennium, please do not hesitate to write me personally:

FOR MEMBERSHIP

Dr. Mushtaq H. Jaafri
919 Sonora Ct.
San Dimas, CA 91773